The Complete IDIOT'S GUIDE to Understanding Support Employees

Leslie D. Lewis

The Unofficial Handbook for Administrative Professionals and the Managers Who Manage Them

The Complete Idiot's Guide to Understanding Support Employees: The Unofficial Handbook for Administrative Professionals and the Managers Who Manage Them

For questions about permissions, bulk orders, or appearances, contact the author at unofficialspeak4support@hotmail.com.

To find out more about how you can fulfill your publishing dream, contact:

Highly Favored Publishing
Bowie, Maryland 20716
(301) 257-6659
highlyfavoredpublishing@gmail.com
www.highlyfavoredpublishing.com
Highly Favored Publishing™ is an entity of Highly Favored, L.L.C.

Printed in the United States of America

ISBN: 978-0-9835157-8-4

Library of Congress Control Number: 2013904821

Barb Stiver

Dedication

To the receptionist,
to the assistant,
to the secretary,
You are my heart!
Keep on surviving!

To my mother,
it might have appeared to go unnoticed,
but I've got it all here in my heart.
I want you to know I know the truth . . .
I would be nothing without you.
You are the wind beneath my wings!
I love you!

To Corey, CJ, & Cori,
being your wife and mommy is the greatest job
I have ever had.
Here's to never quitting, resigning, or transferring.
I love each of you beyond this dedication!

In Memoriam

Daddy,
God promoted you to His office on August 8, 2012.
And while I know you are enjoying
the greatest benefits package ever, it was still too soon.
I love you and I miss you.

Acknowledgments

U.S. Department of Education, Default Management Section (summer 1993), you saw me off to college. Thanks for being my stepping stone. *Eran,* you pretended to be shy really well ☺! *Alekia (Lekie),* the cubicle space was fun because of you. See you both 'round Facebook!

The Pentagon, Office of the Chief of Air Force (summer 1994), you made me feel special. I still have my autographed picture, which is even more special post 9/11. *Deb,* you said you hoped to see me on *The New York Times* best-seller list one day. I'm praying for ANY list ☺! *Mary H.,* I miss ya, Mamá!

Uniformed Services University of the Health Sciences, Research Department (winter break 1994; summer and winter 1995), you are the job I miss the most. I loved the commute, the area, everybody in the office, and the work I had to do. You will always be a special memory because it was here that I met a dear friend.

Lewis J. Ort Library, Acquisitions Department, Frostburg State University (1995-1998), what can I say? You ladies saw the best and worst of me. Thanks for not giving up on me and keeping me employed.

The Lane Center, Frostburg State University (fall semester 1997 to spring semester 1998), this much fun at work should have been against the law! I had an endless supply of popcorn, use of the pool tables in the game room, and got to greet and hang out with the bands and entertainment for school activities. Thanks for the memory of being "Employee of the Month"! (It hasn't happened since ☺.)

Trizechan Office Properties (summer 1998), you were one of the best temp assignments ever. A penthouse office, a beautiful breeze blowing through, laid back, casual staff, lunch on the rooftop with a view of Wisconsin Avenue—wait a minute, are you hiring ☺?

The Willard Intercontinental Hotel, Catering Office (summer 1998), you were another exciting temp assignment and a fun bunch to work around. *Yoko,* I still have the jacket you gave me. I can't believe I was ever your size, girl ☺! Gerald, I was touched when I called the office *six years later* and you remembered me!

Council for Responsible Nutrition (1998-2000), you were my first permanent job after college, and the first job whose mission and purpose I was genuinely interested in. *John Cordaro,* thanks for rescuing me from you know who. I hope I didn't make you too uncomfortable crying in your office. *Ma Vern,* you had me at the interview. Where are you, woman? I miss you.

Kinsella Media, LLC (2000-2002), you will always have my heart! You let me shine! *Kathy,* you could write the book on being a wonderful supervisor because that's what you were. Every job I applied to after Kinsella, I used you as a professional reference, and every employer was compelled to tell me about the "glowing" recommendation you gave each time. Thank you! *Andy,* the hardest working, craziest VP ever! You and Kathy helped us to mature personally and professionally. *Francine,* are you still slugging up and down 495, girl?! Hope you and the family are well. *Huma,* thanks for the laughter on our side of the hall, and for the flowers following my procedure. *Radwa,* the coolest intern ever! Hope you are well . . . daughter ☺!

The Kamber Group Lunch Crew (Andy, Brenda, Christian, Debra, Eric, Jeff, and Marcus), lunchtime was the best time. It's been a *jungle* out here without ya! Haha!

National Captioning Institute (2003), you were my first foot in my dream field. Even though it was only for three months, it was the best three months of my work life!

The Company That Shall Remain Nameless* (TCTSRN) *(2003-2007) . . . *crickets* . . . you killed any joy I ever had for the field of administration. Seriously, you threw it on the floor, stomped on it, and then gave it back to me! *George, Leah, Tomlyne, Wanda, Wyetha, Sherry, Tabatha, Sandra, Larissa, Jerel, Che're, Andy, Christine, Mukhtar, Raymon (RIP), Debbie, and Deborah,* you were all that was cool about TCTSRN. *Wanda,* the moving'est and shaking'est person I know. Your hustle inspires me! It's time you let it inspire the rest of the world! *Tanya S.,* whenever there was an occasion to give toward a gift for us assistants, you were always one of the first to give. Thank you. *Sherry,* you have the greatest personality ever. The way you have remained positive and upbeat through all of your adversity is inspiring. You are a beautiful soul. I am praying for your continued recovery . . . and so is CJ ☺. *Leah,* thank you for the hug when I needed it most. I am eternally grateful for your shoulder and ear that day. Remember when I accidentally sent that e-mail to you know who when we were talking about him?! *still cracking up* *double and triple checking names* *Tomlyne,* my ace on the other side of the hall, my sharer of Take 5's, my chatterbox, my companion to the vending machine and lunch leftovers, my breath of fresh air, my pint-sized angel at TCTSRN (though you killed Percy) . . . I had reached my wit's end when you came, and you kept me company until I broke free ☺! Thank you for being a friend to my family and me. *Since the start of this book, you have been released! Prayerfully, by the time it hits shelves, our favorite vegan will be on the other side as well!*

Department of Transportation, Joint Program Office (2007-2009), it was a hard job restoring some of the love lost for support work, but you succeeded. I will always remember my baby shower. *Kris-*

ty, Tinoula, Demetrius, Esam, Stephen, Debbie, Linda, Kate, RoseMary, thanks for all the great memories. *Zia,* like the saying goes, sometimes it's not what you know, but who you know. Thanks to Leah, I now know my fiery, verbose, opinionated, like-minded twin. Your faith inspires me! Congratulations on your new path. The East Coast will miss you!

Trully & Associates

Trully & Associates
1548 New Birth Street, NW
Third Floor
Washington, DC 20096

MEMORANDUM

April 24, 2013

From: Leslie D. Lewis
To: Joyce M. Trully, President and CEO
Cc: Trully & Associates Staff
Subject: Resignation

From the date of my hire until a few months ago, my employment with Trully & Associates was quite enjoyable. Our working relationship was more than professional; at times, it was personal. And it was pleasant. Now, however, it tinkers on hostile. And it has become difficult for me to hide my displeasure, which, in turn, has created much tension between you, other employees, and me. And rather than continue in this counterproductive manner, effective immediately, I am resigning from my position.

Consequently, you may no longer care about what I have to say, but since it involves the relationship between support and executive staff, I hope you will give these parting thoughts of mine your sincerest attention—despite any hard feelings you may have.

The truth of the matter is, despite the discord that now exists between us, my decision to leave was not an easy one to make. When I accepted this position three years ago, I had already served in a support position for more than seven years—not because I had nothing better to do or wasn't capable of something *greater*, but because I love the field of administration. I adore this work, and contrary to popular opinion, the support position is <u>not</u> the job you *settle for* until something better comes along.

In fact, it is one of the most difficult, most challenging, and sometimes, the most rewarding position a person can have. For years, I enjoyed meeting and exceeding its demands. Unfortunately, my ability to deal professionally with the condescension, double standards, and disrespect shown toward support staff has diminished. I know that patronizing comments, dumb questions, and uncooperative spirits have historically been burdens that assistants must bear, but the day I threw the three-hole punch in your direction, *we both* knew it was time for me to go.

Now, lest I imply that my grief has been all your or someone else's fault, I must say that it has not been. That is why this memorandum is not a mere list of my issues with you. As I resign, the last thing I want is to appear whiny or bitter. Instead, you will find the following:

> **Examples of problematic encounters re-told in their entire context, including the names of all staff involved.** Initially, this may strike you as a form of tattling, but it is not. It is only to ensure that you have the "whole" story, for only when you know the actions and point of view of everyone involved can you understand and perhaps empathize with my frustrations.
>
> Also, **I have provided compromises to each grievance.** Many times, people are quick to express what the problem is, but they never offer a solution. Unfortunately, for many problems in a work environment, absolute solutions are not always possible. So I have offered "compromises" that may at least create a more equitable environment for both management and support employees.

Additionally, **I consciously sought to be open-minded and reasonable in communicating these issues.** Even though I am resigning, I am not bitter and do not harbor any ill feelings toward you or other staff. This writing is not an attempt to "go out with a bang," having painted you or the organization in a negative light. I believe that management's contribution to the grief of the support position is not intentional. It is often inadvertent. Perhaps this is why I have been able to put up with these issues for much of my career.

Finally, as you can see by my CC, I hope you will share this memo with the entire staff. I also hope that should you find this writing sensible, you will forward a copy to other employers, as well. People in support positions are not usually afforded the opportunity to provide this kind of feedback, but as the unofficial spokesperson, I will try to do so now. I am positive the insight you gain will help you better understand "work" from what I believe is an oft-ignored and often misunderstood perspective—the support person's.

Attachments

Attachment One

Creating *False* Emergencies

Stress is basically a disconnection from the earth, a forgetting of the breath. Stress is an ignorant state. It believes that everything is an emergency. Nothing is that important. Just lie down.[1]

- *Natalie Goldberg*

---

[1] "Natalie Goldberg quotes." Accessed March 14, 2013. http://en.thinkexist.com/search/searchQuotation.asp?search=natalie+goldberg.

CONTEXT

Usually, the out-of-state meetings/conferences you attended lasted one or two days, so making your travel arrangements was simple. In December of my first year here, however, you left for a weeklong trip where you attended several meetings. Making your hotel arrangements became a little more involved, as you were preparing to lodge at three different hotels. Making your flight arrangements was also more complicated, but eventually, I secured your reservations and confirmations successfully.

For my own use, I created a "by day" itinerary that reflected your whereabouts as well as your meeting times and locations. When you complemented the format, I explained that if you were needed while away, the itinerary would make it easy to inform staff when you were reachable and where.

***** ***** *****

It had to be close to 5:30 the evening you called and asked me to fax you a copy of an old presentation. You explained that you wanted to have the presentation available as a handout at the next day's meeting.

"Some people from IOP Inc. will be there," you elaborated. "I think I can sneak in a pitch."

We laughed, you thanked me, and I left for the day.

***** ***** *****

The next morning began like any other. I got to my desk at 7:56, set down my Pepsi and my bagel with extra butter, turned on my computer, and prepared to check the messages when you called in a panic.

"Leslie! What happened? I never got the fax!"

"The confirmation sheet is right here," I said casually and pulled it from the machine. "It went through."

"Well, I didn't get it, and I need it for my meeting this morning!"

I glanced at the itinerary and then at the confirmation sheet and saw my mistake. I inadvertently sent the fax to the hotel you checked out of the previous morning.

"Okay, Joyce," I tried to calm you down. "I sent it to JKL Suites instead of RST Hotel. I'm sorry. I'm going to resend it right now. You'll have it in three minutes."

"No! Don't send it to the hotel. I'm already at QWERT's offices."

"Okay, I'll fax it to you there. I have the number."

"Oh, please hurry, Leslie. I want to get some copies made so they can have them at the meeting."

DISCUSSION

I will begin with what I felt justified your hysteria:

1. **You requested and did not receive something needed for a meeting soon to begin.**

2. **That is it!**

Frankly, I did not think you should have been concerned at all. In fact, I was annoyed you acted like the success of your meeting was in jeopardy because you did not have copies of a presentation the night before. Your frenzied tone about a fax that could still get to you in time was stupid. I knew when we hung up the issue was not over. And sure enough, when you returned, you met with me to discuss what you perceived as a nonchalant attitude toward the mistake I had made.

You said: **I should have been more careful and paid closer attention to where the fax was being sent.** If you remember, I agreed with you. I took total responsibility for the oversight. I did not blame it on being in a hurry to leave for the day. Neither did I attribute it to being extremely busy at the time. In fact, I was honest and told you that when you are away, I do play.[2] I admitted I had been playing a game of Words with Friends on my cell phone when you called. You thanked me for my honesty but continued to reprimand me for the mistake.

Had the information become outdated because I sent it to the wrong place? Did the hotel clerk who pulled the misdirected fax work for one of our competitors and suddenly have his hands on a copy of company secrets with which he could take away our members? If not, where was the emergency? Why were you so

[2] I play when you're in the office, too, but I'll get to that later.

panic-stricken as if I couldn't resend the fax to where you were, you make the copies, and you get to your meeting on time?

Nevertheless, I remained silent while you went on to express your surprise behind my "flippant" attitude. "You completely acted like nothing was wrong, Leslie." I explained that according to my itinerary, your meeting wasn't for another two hours. I wasn't unconcerned about my mistake; I just thought I had more than enough time to get the presentation faxed to you.

Then, you informed me: **The meeting was moved up to 8:00 a.m., and because you did not have the fax in time, the meeting started about 10 minutes late.** Joyce, did the attendees get up and leave, refuse to even hear your presentation, because you had the audacity to start late? Did you become the first executive in corporate history NOT to begin a meeting on time? Was everyone even there by 8:00? No one even knew about this particular handout. Yes, it was late getting faxed to you, and yes, the copies were late getting made. Was their distribution the first item on the agenda?

I know this sounds very arrogant, but my point is only that the situation was not critical. There was no reason for you to act like the company was going bankrupt, and I was responsible. In two years, I have made other mistakes that, to me, weren't serious either. But judging from your (over)reaction, you disagreed then, too.

FALSE EMERGENCIES

I neglected to order more coffee when ordering food and supplies for the kitchens (break rooms): And it just so happened that four representatives from SDF Masters, Inc. were coming that morning for a meeting. You became very uptight behind the fact that we had no coffee to offer them. For 10 minutes, you opened and slammed the kitchen drawers and cabinets, mumbling (loud enough for everyone to hear), "I can't believe we don't have any coffee in this whole damn place!"

I wished that a box of spoons or something had fallen on your head! It was four people for goodness' sake. Two people were already drinking coffee when they arrived; the Starbucks across the street sufficed for another; and one gentleman wanted water, anyway. Later, I placed an order for coffee, and it was in the office the next day.

I neglected to specify "3-hole paper" on the copy form upon dropping off material to the copy center: The material was for the 40 binders we had to make for the next morning's board meeting. When Monica returned the box to my desk, you remained there for your copy. When you saw the job had been copied on regular, un-punched paper, you threw the copy down on my desk, rolled your eyes, and stomped back to your office.

I wasn't *really* aiming for the floor when I threw that three-hole punch! An inconvenience, yes. But an emergency? NO! Jacob, Shaun, Kia, and I formed a little assembly line in the conference room, and we three-hole punched the copies, assembled the notebooks, and had fun doing it. That is what that little contraption is for, by the way. Because of their help, we finished in no time, and I was still able to go home on time. (And FYI: if you had accidentally hit me with those papers, I *would have* thrown the machine dead at your head!)

I transferred a call to your desk and identified the caller incorrectly: I told you that "Marilyn" was on the line when her name was actually "Carolyn." You picked up the phone and sang, "Hellooo, Marilyn." For the rest of the day everyone heard how embarrassed you were that the president of BNM United, our newly acquired member, had to correct you.

crickets

Did she hang up because you called her Marilyn? Curse you out? Withdraw their membership? I guess you would have never confused those two names, huh? I wasn't on the phone, but I'm almost certain she wasn't upset or offended. (And if she was, then YOU should have hung up on HER!)

I neglected to indicate "no cheese" on the sandwich ordered for the chairman of the board: During lunch, he peeled back the wrapper, noticed the cheese, and immediately made his irritation known. You brought the sandwich to where I sat across the room, pointed to the cheese, and in front of the entire board room, yelled, "How could you have forgotten to say no cheese!"

$!@#%

First of all, did it ever occur to you that I <u>had</u> requested no cheese and that the <u>vendor</u> made a mistake? Second, that man makes well over six figures. As far as I was concerned, he could have taken his cheap butt across the street and gotten something else to eat, removed the cheese from the FREE sandwich, or CHOSEN ANOTHER SANDWICH!

At most, these mistakes caused some embarrassment, inconvenience, or aggravation for all involved, but not one was a catastrophe. Not one called for any ranting or raving, whooping and hollering, hand waving, eye rolling, head shaking, hip holding, arm crossing, heavy sighing, light swearing, lengthy staring, foot stomping, or teeth clenching on your part. This is not to say, however, that such "carrying on" is never justified. There are times when these and other behaviors are more than appropriate.

I accidentally send confidential information for Boyd Corporation to Clemson, LLC: Boyd has every right to be upset, to consider the company incompetent, and to withdraw their membership. Clemson may worry that we could get as careless with their confidential information and withdraw their membership, as well.

I fail to catch inaccurate amounts in a cost spreadsheet: The line item should read $1,000,000. Instead, $1,000 gets entered; an invoice is generated and sent to the client. The error is exposed—by the client, no less—and we have to eat the cost, or hope they will allow us to generate a revised invoice and pay the real cost.

The true crises that these mistakes create should be obvious: money and members are lost, the company appears inept, and our reputation is severely damaged. Surely, you can "carry on" behind these things, and I will even agree that such mistakes can be grounds for termination (especially if they occur frequently). The point, however, is that more mistakes are minor than major, and they are not as catastrophic as your reaction sometimes implies.

For example, we sent an electronic notice about last month's Power Summit to the board of directors and several committees. The date of the summit was April 20, and in closing the e-mail, I asked that people "RSVP to me no later than Friday, March 15." Well, the e-mail was sent on March 28, so I should have written *April* 15. In a matter of minutes, the error was brought to my attention by several members who replied to tell me that I meant April 15.

It was very annoying to have half the list respond to point out my mistake, but not to indicate whether they were attending! I had to write back to each of them: "Thank you for bringing that oversight to my attention. I will amend the e-mail shortly. In the meantime, however, should I count your response as an RSVP, or will you be unable to attend the Power Summit?" *Jackass!*

If the recipients could not figure out what the date should have been, that's a stupidity they have to live with. I did not want to send another e-mail at all, but I knew you would expect me to. I was already preparing the text when you came running to my desk waving a copy of the e-mail in the air. "Leslie! Leslie! You have to get this out again! We have to get it out again! The date is wrong! Oh my goodness!"

For a second, I thought the building was on fire and you were yelling for us to get out and save ourselves! You could have calmly said, "Leslie, you need to resend the e-mail. The RSVP date was wrong." Close to 150 people were invited, and more than 100 came. And while I could tell that you were pleased with the turnout, I remember you made it a point to "joke" with the members about the miswritten e-mail.

Did my mistake embarrass the company that badly, Joyce? Do you think members went home that evening and talked about you, the company, or me over dinner? Half of those you spoke to didn't even remember the "fiasco." It was a mistake for goodness' sake, and similar to the phone list episode, it wasn't even a serious one.

On my first day at Trully, my very first "assignment" was to update the employee phone list. Just prior to my coming, there had been about three other new hires, as well, and you asked me to update the phone list with each of our names. You even commented, "I realize this is just busy work, but until we get you set up on the network, it's something to kill some time."

I was actually grateful for that "busy work," and to kill more time, I entered the information in table form, which it previously had not been. After lunch, when John finished my computer set-up, I printed the contact list and personally delivered a copy to everyone. This was another attempt to kill time as well as an opportunity to begin putting a face to people's names.

Before I could even return to my desk, Gordon found me hanging a list in the first break room. "What is it again, Lisa?"

"Leslie."

"Lez-lee, my extension is wrong. You have six-nine-zero-two, but it's six-nine-*two-zero,*" he emphasized like I had suddenly become dumb or hard of hearing.

In hindsight, I recognize this as the handwriting on the wall concerning my relationship with Gordon. Recounting this now actually makes me laugh because here was a man—his vice presidency irrelevant—throwing a fit because his extension was incorrect on a friggin *internal* staff list! I did not know Gordon then, so his behavior surprised me. Now, however, I know that it would not have mattered if the mistake were on something for the board, something internal, or something for his eyes only because he overreacted even when there was no mistake!

Take our committee work, for example. I know every company's "business" is different, so their day-to-day is different. For us, committee work was a major component, and as a result, we could have anywhere from four to ten committee meetings a week. It was not uncommon to have up to three meetings in one day. The committees that Jacob and I primarily supported depended on the managers we supported. Though we were the administrative contacts for different committees, the prep work we completed for any committee meeting was the same.

We had to take RSVPs and order lunch accordingly; electronically distribute the meeting agenda and any other handouts/materials in advance of the meeting (as well as upload materials to the committee website); ascertain from the agenda and/or communication with the manager if there were any presentations, and if so, have them cued on the computer; set up any audio or video equipment, if needed; create a sign-in sheet; and make sure there were extra copies of the agenda and other meeting materials available.

There were a lot of small tasks and responsibilities but nothing requiring a doctoral degree. Jacob and I prepared for meetings all day, every day. We could prepare for a meeting in our sleep . . . which is why Gordon aggravated the hell out of me when he asked before each meeting if I had done these things! Oh, how I hated his face at my desk the day of a meeting. "Leslie, did you remember the extra copies of the agenda?" "Leslie, don't forget the sign-in sheet." "Is the presentation on the computer yet?" Seriously, if I didn't know how to prepare for a committee meeting—at least, after the millionth one—I should have been fired a long time ago!

Certainly, supporting our membership and being prepared went a long way in making our company look good, but these meetings were not so serious that he had to panic before each one. Even if it was a board of directors meeting, for which *you* especially became a pain, it was not an emergency. I did not need to be asked every time if I had remembered to do what I had known to do *all* the other times.

Gordon even managed to turn organizing the supply closets into some major undertaking. The simple labels Jacob and I created made a world of difference in what was previously an unorganized blob of supplies. The labels, of course, were in addition to arranging supplies by type, straightening up, and storing loose and excess items in a container or bin. At the subsequent staff meeting, following your quick "thank you both for getting those closets together without even being asked," he passed out a friggin "map" of the closets with his suggestions for a revised layout. I was beyond annoyed reading his ideas to put the black and blue pens on this shelf and all the other color pens on that shelf; put the mechanical pencils in this color bin and the other pencils in that color bin; face the legal accordion folders on the shelf this way and the legal manila folders that way . . .

Even *you* stuttered slightly when it came time to respond because you knew his proposal was re-damn-diculous! But, of course, you never said anything. Instead, you "co-signed" that foolishness and allowed him to dictate a due date by which we had to make the supply closets comply. Following the meeting, however, Jacob and I decided that we were not changing anything.

Aside from the fact that the closets were a grand mess before we took it upon ourselves to organize them, retrieving supplies from a supply closet—we thought—was as idiot-proof as any procedure could be. It did not require a color illustration or labels with color text to match the color of supplies they identified, or any of the other nonsense he wanted.

People are still talking about the day he asked us to come with him to one of the closets. This was after he had voiced his dissatisfaction with how we had not yet incorporated his changes, "when [I gave] them to [you] more than three weeks ago." In particular, his suggestion to remove all generic labels (such as notepads, staples, pens, etc.) and create individual labels that also identified a supply's size, color, etc. (such as *legal-size* notepads, *letter-size* notepads, *red* pens, or *blue* pens).

He swung open one of the closets and then stepped to the side.

"Now, if I need a box of small paper clips, what do I do? How do I find them?"

I REFUSED to answer and stood in silence. After a few seconds of silence, Jacob took up the challenge. "The label says 'paper clips,' Gordon."

"Exactly. It *only* says 'paper clips,'" he retorted. "How can I tell if these are small, medium, or large paper clips?"

"Wouldn't you just look on the box?" Jacob asked. "Or am I missing something?"

"I'm missing lunch," I interrupted, and left.

Figure 1.

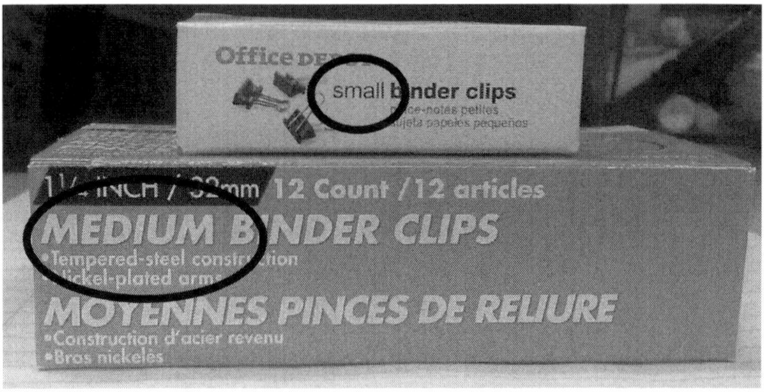

Do I even have to explain?

COMPROMISE

When a mistake is made, employers should first determine whether that mistake is a catastrophe or an inconvenience. Employers might ask themselves: *Is my reputation as president of this company permanently blemished? Can we lose membership behind this mistake? Will this adversely affect our earnings or revenue?* If the answer is no, then it is likely not serious, and you should act accordingly. To react otherwise creates unnecessary tension and could lead to more mistakes or, worse, alienation.

If you send something to the printer and find it did not print because I neglected to fill the paper tray, by all means, be annoyed. But please tell me what you accomplish by sighing loudly, flinging open the tray, and stuffing paper into it? The tray gets filled, yes, but the dramatics—aside from giving me something else to talk about during lunch—cause me to become so tense about that one thing that I may overlook something else. Perhaps I begin to focus more on the paper tray and forget to change Chairman Brown's fax number in the database. At least then, when you print the *outdated* roster, there will be paper in the printer. Or, maybe I will never forget to order coffee again, but I forget the filters. These examples might seem a stretch, but it can be counterproductive to make a big deal out of little things. Therefore, employers should make a conscious effort to recognize what the little things are.

Also, when you carry on behind insignificant mistakes, staff can lose the motivation to do good work because employers don't at least appreciate the effort that was made. Therefore, you might also consider: *Is this behavior or mistake typical of my assistant?* If you had to reprimand daily an employee for sloppy, erroneous work, then "overreacting" would make sense. But when mistakes are few and far between, such hysterics only alienate the employee from the employer.

Case in point, last month's special staff meeting. You were in a very good mood. We had acquired three new clients in two weeks, which gave us five plans to work on at one time. Though we were very busy, it also meant $5 million in commission, so we did not mind. Everyone joked openly about Christmas bonuses looking good!

In lieu of our regular staff meeting, you called an impromptu meeting to discuss the workload. You asked me to print and have copies of:

- the budget and paid media sections for the Juvenile Centers plan;
- the background for the Cities plan;
- the website section for the Davidson Funeral Home plan;
- the methodology section for the Cinema, Inc. Plan; and
- the budget for the Gyms of America plan.

You wanted to discuss the Cinema, Inc. plan first, so you asked me to hand out copies of the methodology. It only took me a minute to browse through my paper-clipped stack to realize I had forgotten to print it. When my omission was obvious, you jumped up from the table and returned 15 minutes later with your stack of the same information, but including the methodology section. You took your seat and sighed, "Now that I know everything is here, we can begin."

Immediately following the meeting, I told you I was going home because I was not feeling well.

"Suddenly, huh?" you asked.

"Suddenly," I replied, said goodbye to Jacob and left.

I called in sick the next two days without any remorse for the fact that we were busy. I was very angry and hurt by your reaction. I resented your reaction. Was my omission that serious, Joyce? You couldn't move on to discuss another plan while I stepped out to make the copies? It was an internal meeting for goodness' sake. I know you had an order to the information you wanted to present, but would it have killed you to reverse the first two items? Who would have known? Who would have *cared*?

Compared to the complexity of the request itself and the extraordinary amount of work we had coming up, my omission was minor—on some levels, comical even. I half expected to hear, "Well, if this is any sign of how well we'll do with all this work, we're in trouble!" Even that would have been better than how you reacted. I had everything else copied and ready for you, but you chose to throw a tantrum behind the one thing I missed.

SUMMARY

I know the importance of quality work and how easily a company's reputation can be damaged by mistakes. I also know the affect this could have on membership, which in turn affects revenue, and the snowball keeps going. However, mistakes are going to happen. From the ownership level down to the intern, they cannot be avoided. Rather than raise your blood pressure behind each one, worry only about those that warrant concern: those that affect your reputation, revenue, or membership. If a mistake has not negatively affected any of these things, then react accordingly.

First, one must consider an employee's work history. Is this particular mistake, or mistakes period, common to your employee? If mistakes are not common, act like they are not. Do not react as if an employee consistently performs poorly if he or she does not. You might repeat the instructions and your desired outcome to your employee, but just like the "time should fit the crime," your reaction should be comparable to whatever has taken place.

Second, when you consider the operation of an organization as a whole, how serious is it that one day you don't have coffee to offer visitors? Can you not function the rest of the day because your assistant incorrectly assumed you were away from your desk and sent your husband to your voicemail? Are these omissions, mistakes, and oversights more important than having a database you can trust is always current? Or having office equipment that is rarely out of order because maintenance and service are closely monitored?

Employers should not create an atmosphere where employees are scared to death of messing up. An environment that is unnecessarily too intense can make employees uncomfortable. Some may become overwhelmed by the pressure and begin making additional mistakes. Others can resent the unnecessarily demanding environment and lose motivation to do good work for fear it won't be satisfactory anyway.

Finally, managers ought to avoid creating an atmosphere of "my way or the highway." Imposing your way on employees just because you are the manager is not wise. What is wise is to acknowledge that good ideas and good work can come from employees in any position. Everyone contributes something worthwhile to an organization.

Attachment Two

Misplacing Blame

To err is human, to blame the next guy even more so.[3]

– *Unknown*

[3] "Unknown: To err is human, to blame the next guy even more so." Accessed January 11, 2013. http://www.quotes.net/quote/42065.

CONTEXT

A few months ago, you and I were in your office going over the particulars for a conference call.

"Who else from here will participate?" I asked.

"It'll be me, John, Jeff, and Cecilia. You can ask Justin and Carl if they want to sit in, but they don't have to."

"Okay."

"And it's just the executive board members. It'll be a one-agenda-item conference call to discuss and vote on going after the Farmers case."

"Okay. So the quorum will be . . . 11?"

"Yes. Five manufacturer and six distributor companies should be represented."

You left early that day, and by the next morning, I had e-mailed you a copy of the results spreadsheet. In it, I captured the names of the attendees, the five date options, and any qualifying notes. We laughed together at Justin not being available on either of the Friday dates. "No surprise there," you chuckled.

By mid-morning, the polling was complete, and before I left for lunch, I sent an e-mail to everyone indicating the conference call would be on Thursday, November 6, 2008. I included the dial-in number and instructions, provided the background on the agenda item, and repeated that there would be a vote taken. I listed the attendees who would participate, and since the call was four days away, I announced that for good measure, I would overnight hard copies of the same information to each participant.

*****   *****   *****

On the day of the conference call, several people called me instead of the call-in number; some never connected at all because they were waiting to be called; and others forgot about the call altogether. There were only three people besides our staff who connected.

You apologized and let everyone know that due to lack of a quorum, the call would be rescheduled. You excused everyone from the conference room, buzzed me at my desk, and asked me to join you there. On my way, Cecilia stopped me in the hallway and gave me a quick rundown of what had happened, so I knew where the conversation was likely headed. Or rather, I knew who was about to be blamed.

I took my seat across from you and watched you stare blankly into the air for five minutes before sighing heavily. And sure enough, you asked, "What did you do?"

DISCUSSION

The majority of the answers I wanted to give were rude. Misplacing blame is a great source of my resentment toward executive staff. If you had asked me, "What happened?" the implication would not have necessarily been that it was my fault, but you blamed me first, immediately. I actually thought we might have a good laugh at members' inability to follow directions, but apparently, the joke was on me. At any rate, to answer your question, here is what I did:

On Friday, October 31, I sent:

EXECUTIVE BOARD MEMBERS:

Thank you for your cooperation in providing your availability for an emergency teleconference. Based on your responses, a conference call has been scheduled for **Thursday, November 6, 2008, from 10:00 a.m. – 11:00 a.m., EST.**

CALL PURPOSE:

On Thursday, November 6, 2008, from 10 a.m. – 11 a.m., members and staff will participate in a one-hour conference call. **A vote will be taken** on making a bid for the Farmers case. Attached for your information is background on the Farmers of Mountainous America.

CALL PARTICULARS:

You are expected to dial into the conference call. The dial-in number is 1-888-555-5555, and the pass code is 888. If you have any questions, please contact Joyce at (202) 555-5555, or at joyce.trully@trullyandassociates.org. Hard copies of these instructions and the background will be sent overnight.

Again, we have had our share of laughs at how ridiculous members can be sometimes, and after I recap for you everything that went wrong, you may be able to see why I was prepared to laugh again.

☎ **Members called the office instead of dialing into the conference call directly.**

Joyce, under "Call Particulars," the first line said they were required to dial in. How some of them read this and still interpreted it to mean we would call them, I do not know. Would we have given a dial-in number if we were going to call? I know we usually called everyone, but this is why paying attention is important. I have my own DUH moments to worry about. I cannot worry about and be responsible for others', too.

Chairman Burr especially pissed me off when he called my line and nastily asked me what the hell the hold up was. "I've been sitting here ten minutes waiting for you to call me. What are you doing over there?" In the politest voice I could muster at the time, I replied: "Chairman Burr, you were supposed to dial-in, so actually, I'm wondering what the hell *you're* doing!"

Okay, of course I did not say that, but I would not have been out of line if I had. He never even apologized for his misplaced accusation. Instead, he demanded, "Connect me, now!"

Furious, I pressed TRANSFER as hard as I could and walked to the conference room to see if he had connected okay. By the time I came back to my desk, four more people had left messages asking why we had not called them yet. By the time I called each of them back, the call was over and *they* were upset.

☎ **Members forgot about the conference call.**

I remember you asking me with visible irritation, "Okay, how did you notify them again?"

It took everything in me not to explode. "I sent an e-mail—you were copied on it—that stated the date three times. And then I sent hard copies to their offices, as well."

When you asked me if that was all, I lost it. "Yes, that is all, Joyce. If I tell someone something six times and they still forget, what do you think I can do about it?"

At that moment, I would not have cared if you had shaken your head completely off your neck! It was my job to adequately inform members of the call, and I had done that. It was NOT my job nor in my power to make them **remember** the call, too!

Worst of all, however, were the truants who remembered the call and knew to dial in, but still did not connect because they had the "wrong number."

☎ Members dialed the "wrong number."

I think what shocked me most about this excuse was that my favorite member, Secretary Green, used it. One of the main members needed on the call sent an e-mail to the entire board expressing his "outrage" at being sent the wrong number. As sad as I was that dear Secretary Green had not "gotten it," I was even sadder when you acted like he had a point!

I did not draft and send different e-mails to members, Joyce. Secretary Green received the same number that everyone else did. What he should have said, and what you should have realized, was that he misdialed. He was so used to having a particular dial-in number that he had not taken the time to realize the number was different for this call. Just how long was he going to keep dialing the "wrong" number, anyway?

COMPROMISE

Misplacing blame is probably the most personal issue, and though the suggestions I offer may appear childish, I hope the seriousness of my point will not be undermined. To my detriment, I am an idealist and very fairytale-minded, believing that no matter the office hierarchy—everyone deserves respect and fairness. As naïve as this sounds, when people do not get either, especially those in a support position, it makes me angry.

The poster I kept over my desk, "All I Really Need to Know I Learned in Kindergarten,"[4] comes closest to describing my sentiments surrounding this issue.

☺ **Remember the Dick-and-Jane books and the first word you learned—the biggest word of all—LOOK!**

You were copied on the e-mail I sent to the executive board members. Before you started flinging accusations, did you even LOOK first to determine what had happened? If you had taken time to examine things, you would have already known why the call failed and that it was through no fault of mine. Of course, this was not the only time you neglected to properly LOOK at a situation or information.

You might remember last year's holiday party when you asked me to keep a running RSVP list. After I created and saved it, I sent you an e-mail with the file name and location. If I had a dollar for every time you asked me what the numbers looked like, instead of looking yourself, I could have eaten lunch for a week in our cafeteria! Why did you even ask me to create the document if you were not going to look at it? I know it was easier to call me versus finding

---

[4] Fulghum, Robert. "All I Really Need to Know I Learned in Kindergarten," Accessed February 3, 2011, http://www.kalimunro.com/learned_in_kindergarten.html.

and opening it yourself, but from where I sat, it was also very lazy. My title was administrative "*assist*ant," not administrative "*be-interrupted-50-times-a-day-to-answer-questions-your-boss-can-answer-if-she-just-looked-herself*tant!"

Again, such a position might seem arrogant to you. After all, I was the assistant, and I know that sometimes meant accommodating your own laziness and vanity insofar as being the president was concerned. However, there were times when your laziness and vanity were out of line and bordered on abuse (a point on which I will elaborate in a later section).

In the e-mail I sent for the holiday party, I bolded, italicized, and highlighted instructions to ***RSVP to me*** by Friday, December 5, 2007. I guess I should have underlined it too. Not only did half the members send their RSVP to you, but some sent it to all 350 people on the distribution list. You scared me half to death when you stormed out of your office and up to my desk, yelling at the top of your lungs about all of the RSVPs flooding your inbox. Had you LOOKED first, you would have seen that I did ask people to RSVP to me. Was it really my fault that people did not know the difference between REPLY and REPLY ALL? I had even suggested to you prior to sending the e-mail that we make the list blind to prevent this very thing, but noooooooo! You insisted that everyone's name be visible. So, arguably, it was *your* fault that every two minutes a box popped up on your screen announcing that somebody was or was not coming.

In other instances, why did I have to stop working to tell you which committee someone was on when you could have LOOKED in the committee notebook I created and kept in your office? Why did I have to be interrupted every time you needed a fax number when you were capable of LOOKING for the number yourself in your Outlook contacts folder? I know being a manager—in this case, the president—came with a lot of prerogatives, but taking advantage of my position was not one of them. Neither was blaming me for things over which I had no control.

How many times did you harass me behind the late delivery of lunch? When did I gain the ability to move cars and eliminate traffic so the delivery guy could arrive on time, Joyce? Was I supposed to go to the store and help make the sandwiches, too, or should I have demanded that vendors not accept any other orders on the days we had deliveries?

Of course, I'm being condescending, but my point is that we could have specified any time we wanted. There was no guarantee that it would never come late. For one reason or another, it happened. You did not have to pace back and forth in front of my desk, or in and out of the conference room, agitated and uptight. You did not have to ask me 10 times if I was sure I said 11:30, especially when none of those theatrics ever resulted in lunch coming any sooner!

On occasion, you even behaved like malfunctioning AV equipment was my fault, too. It wasn't! I know it annoyed you when the laptop or projector broke, especially during or right before the more important meetings, but was that my fault? No, you never came out and said, "Leslie, this is your fault." But how else was I to interpret your eye rolling and piercing stares while I fiddled with the machines to get them working again, or switched them out? Did you think I had taken a bat to the machines the night before just so they would not work for your meeting?

You think I liked dealing with you when you were in that kind of mood? Yes, your heart was set on watching the pretty slides on the high-end projector with the cool, animated graphics, but sometimes, you just needed to make do without that—and *not* because I had done anything wrong!

☺ **Say you're sorry when you hurt somebody.**

I do not know why people find this simple appeal so hard, but I imagine pride has a lot to do with it. In an office environment, in particular, managers sometimes reason (and faultily so) that there are "big I's" (them) and "little you's" (the support). While they may not be so bold as to express this opinion verbally, their actions are loud enough.

I cannot help but feel fresh hurt every time I remember the way you screamed at me after the RSVP incident. The fact that I was not even at fault was one thing, but to scream so violently at me *without an eventual apology* was another. Now, deep down I know you were not actually upset because people were RSVPing to you and not to me. We all had private issues we carried around and quietly tried to deal with on the job. Sometimes, when we tried to juggle those personal stressors on top of work frustrations, the result was a short fuse set off by the littlest things. We all had moments when we took private matters out on someone else.

In fact, during many of our "friendlier" moments, we confided some very personal things in each other—things I never shared with anyone else out of respect for you and the camaraderie we did have on occasion. So when others came to me after your blow-up asking, "What was that all about?" I pretended to be just as oblivious. I knew you were venting a personal issue, and I needed to shake off your behavior. However, it still hurt that you never apologized. I deserved an apology. You would have never talked that way to Gordon, Chairman Burr, or any of the other "big I's."

Just a few weeks ago, when you were rushing home, you asked me to send the draft meeting summary for the last Compensation Committee meeting. On your way out of the door, you stopped at my desk and explained that you had just e-mailed the minutes to me. You asked me to get them out to the committee as soon as possible. We watched together as your e-mail popped up. I said okay, and you left. It only took a minute to click FORWARD, add the appropriate distribution list, remove your text to me, and hit SEND.

When I came in the next morning, your note in my chair greeted me. "Please see me." Jacob and I exchanged smiles, and I journeyed to your office. As soon as I appeared in your doorway, you started.

"Leslie, what did I ask you to do yesterday when I left?"

"Send out the summary for the last Comp Committee meeting."

"And did you do that?"

Did you LOOK in your inbox? "I copied you on the e-mail, Joyce. Yes, I sent it."

"You sent the wrong attachment, Leslie! You should have sent May's minutes. I came in this morning to seven messages from members telling me that you sent the wrong attachment."

"I sent what you e-mailed me, Joyce." I crossed the room to your computer, opened your SENT folder, and as animated as I could, circled your *March* summary attachment with the cursor. When I was confident that you had realized *your* mistake, I closed the folder.

"All I did was click FORWARD and send out what you had attached."

I lost my breath when you spoke again.

"Leslie, I need an assistant who is going to go the extra mile sometimes and not just do what she's told. You knew what month's summary it should have been. So it would have behooved you to double-check the attachment and not be so quick to 'just hit send,'" you mocked me. "Please send the right attachment now."

You might remember that Jacob ended up resending this particular e-mail because I politely left your office, grabbed my things, and left. How in the hell could you think that was my fault, or rather mine alone? There was definitely some validity to me taking my time. I remember enough occasions where my haste caused mistakes that could have been avoided had I slowed down, but you never once acknowledged that you *had* sent me the wrong attachment.

Whether I should have double-checked what *you* had done or not, I half expected to hear, "I'm sorry, Leslie. I did attach the wrong thing, but . . . ." To blame only me and never admit your part in it was not just wrong, it was hypocritical, also. Weren't *you* rushing, too, which is the reason you sent the wrong attachment? So shouldn't *you* have double-checked your work, also? Shouldn't *you* have shared in the blame for this incident like you should have for the power booklet?

You recall the power booklet, right? Monica compiled the information, and you gave it to me to create a four-panel booklet. This became a two-week project as information was added and deleted, graphics were changed, and color schemes modified. Between you, Monica, and me, we looked at the booklet more times than I can count. When it eventually met your approval, you sent out a staff-wide e-mail acknowledging my creativity and work on it.

I thanked you privately for the opportunity to showcase the other abilities of mine that extend beyond usual administrative work. I was quite excited that something I had designed received so many compliments. When I learned the booklet would be placed on our website and made available to the public and all of our members, I was thrilled! On the day of the board meeting, it was Jacob who noticed our zip code was wrong.

Initially, I intended to use this as an example of a "false emergency" because the website version had not gone live yet. This meant we had time to make the change before uploading it. On top of that, 90% of the people downloading or ordering the booklet would be members and would not be looking at the address anyway. I would have been surprised if they noticed the error themselves. Even where non-members were concerned, if they had used the incorrect zip code on the booklet to mail their order or payment to the office, we would have still received the mail. Even more, this is the age of the World Wide Web. Not many people would be sending requests by postal mail, anyway. As far as I was concerned, the incorrect zip code was not earth shattering and was not going to affect much. But I knew you would not see it that way, and I braced myself for the blame that did come the next morning.

My point again: didn't you look at the brochure, i.e., our address and zip code, as many times as I did? Didn't you fail to catch the mistake, as well? Couldn't this have been something we laughed about, fixed, and then went on with our lives?

☺ **When you go out into the world, watch out for traffic, hold hands, and stick together.**

Membership is basically the same everywhere. There are members you absolutely love and some who can drive you to drinking, especially when it comes to delusions of grandeur. If you will bear with me, I would like to take my time discussing this point.

Personally, I do not think members are deluded at all. They are quite aware of their meaningless existence, so they act like mean-spirited, spoiled children to vent the hurt of that realization. They make some of the dumbest, most aggravating requests and demands because they can. They have no authority or influence anywhere else, so they abuse the superficial authority that a member-based organization provides. Consider these things that I had to remember:

> One group wanted more diet sodas while the next group preferred more regular; one group even preferred more Pepsi® while the next more Coke®; one committee wanted its tent cards prepared in Times New Roman, but another found Arial easier to read; one committee was always hot and requested the temperature be lower than usual, and behind them came another committee who could not get warm enough to save their lives; one chairman needed the soft-bottom, swivel chair, but another chairman absolutely had to have the hard-bottom folding chair; one group of committee members liked the blue, gel-ink rollerball pens, and the next group could not seem to function unless they had the black, retractable ballpoint pens.

Understand that I do not have a problem with people being comfortable, having back problems, watching calories, and the like. We all have a right to preferences and quirks, but let me continue:

> One committee liked electronic correspondence while another insisted they receive hard copies of everything; when an attachment was more than 20KB, one chairman demanded I send it to his work e-mail address, but all other e-mails and attachments could be sent to his Hotmail address; mail sent to another chairman was to go to her VA office on Mondays, Wednesdays, and Fridays and to her DC office on Tuesdays and Thursdays; correspondence about the Power Committee was to be mailed to one member's home, while mail concerning

the Compensation Committee needed to be mailed to his office; and let's not forget individual committee preferences for e-mails to be typed in Arial, 12 pt. for one, Tahoma, 11pt. for another, Century Schoolbook, 12 pt. for another, and so forth.

I accepted that the majority of our members were elected officials who conducted business from multiple locations, and I understood that because their (and other members') schedules were fast-paced and always changing, I needed to be flexible and very organized in providing support to them. However—and I'm asking you—why couldn't they impart some of that same understanding to me knowing the challenge it was to support them? Ultimately, I realize this is more a rhetorical question than anything else, but it is a serious one the same. Not every member was a pain, but all of Trully and Associates knew who our "problem children" were. I know for a fact that you, too, were annoyed reading e-mails about there being too many mixed juice drinks instead of plain juice drinks. When board Vice Chairman Brown asked if we could find tablets with a back other than cardboard because it felt funny against his hand, tell me you didn't want to haul off and smack him, too!

When Ms. Wells, God bless her, during the questions and answers period at the Water Workshop, asked why the tablets were yellow when there are white, pink, and other colors available, I know I wasn't the only one who wished she could have shoved one of the tablets down her throat! Experts had flown in from all over the country and had just finished some very dynamic presentations, and she raised her hand to ask about tablets?

Of all the "preferences" I had to remember and satisfy—sensible and stupid—couldn't you understand why after a point, I just didn't give a good goddamn if I forgot to say no cheese on a sandwich and somebody got mad? Or how I could care less about running out of yellow tablets, forcing a committee to use white ones instead? When I mistakenly sent the board notebook to Mr.

Shin's VA office instead of his DC office (because it was Tuesday and not Wednesday), you really could not comprehend why I did not move any faster to courier another copy to the right office when the board meeting wasn't for another week, anyway? Some days, Joyce, I did not care at all about tablets, cords, the temperature, or lunch, but I always cared that you never spoke up for me.

I waited many times for some sort of support from you. Just once, I wanted to see an e-mail from you saying, "Look, I think *we* have more important things to worry about than tablets being legal-size and not letter-size." I might have been able to bear more if you had responded to Mr. Shin's e-mail and stressed—professionally, of course—that what mattered was that he got the notebook! "We do not have time to worry about which office you're in today. You do not need the material for another week, anyway. Get it when you get back to the VA office tomorrow, and SHUT UP!"

I'm being facetious, but I think you understand my point. Sometimes, you would come to my desk, and we would share laughs about these "ridiculous" e-mails and members. We shared a real long laugh about Senator Redd, who stopped her committee meeting to ask why there were more fruit juices than sodas. Even you took that opportunity to mock the way she stood up and pounded on the desk. But when she sent an irate e-mail blasting me about it, with the whole committee CC'd, I waited and waited for some reply from you on my behalf . . . but you never said anything.

SUMMARY

My fault or your fault—the need to discern such might seem childish, but in an environment where *individuals* are recognized for their successes or failures, fault especially becomes a sensitive issue. If the entire company were reprimanded for a mistake, there may not have been a need for this discussion. However, pointing the finger at the *person* deemed responsible creates the need to defend because let's face it, no one wants to be the reason something goes wrong. No one wants to be falsely accused, either, and it is the misfortune of assistants to be blamed first, or entirely, when something goes wrong.

This tendency can be avoided if managers first remember that many of the administrative assistant's responsibilities involve the contribution or involvement of other staff. Instead of jumping immediately to the conclusion that "the assistant did it," consider the event in its entirety and seek to know the involvement of everyone concerned. If an assistant has entered the wrong fax number into the database, do not blow up before you learn that she entered what someone else gave her. If a vendor has delivered the wrong supplies, or if something is missing, investigate before accusing. Look at the purchase order first and see that the item was ordered, but the vendor neglected to deliver it. When managers take the time to do this, only then can blame be accurately assigned.

Managers should also keep in mind that for some things, no one is to blame, least of all the assistant. If a committee insists that lunch be set up after the meeting is already in progress (because the aroma of the food is distracting when set-up in advance), but then complains that there is too much noise when putting the potato chips on the table, why are you angry with the assistant? She has no control over the sound that cellophane makes. She has not deliberately tried to be noisy, but bottled drinks, which a committee insists on having mind you, are going to make some noise—so the distraction can actually be considered their fault (if fault must be assigned).

Managers must also be mindful of the daunting task it is to support an office and its membership. Supporting an office internally comes with its own priorities and demands. When you add the eccentricities and idiosyncrasies of membership, the challenge can become excessive and mentally draining. Assistants are more than capable of handling this challenge, but just as we try to look out for the rest of the office and our membership, sometimes we need you to look out for us.

Sometimes, we need you to apologize when you are wrong, and you *are* wrong sometimes. Being the boss means that you are the boss. It does not mean that you are always right. Consideration should be given because some situations are only disguised home issues that unfortunately seep out into the work place, but at the end of the day, no one is better than anyone. I understand that "totem poles" will probably exist forever in an office, and unfortunately, support staff will likely always be at the bottom. However, management would be wise to remember that when the bottom crumbles, it takes everything else down with it.

Attachment Three

Asking *Annoying* Questions

There are no stupid questions but there are a LOT of inquisitive idiots.[5]

– *Unknown*

[5] Despair, Inc., "Cluelessness." Accessed March 22, 2013. http://www.despair.com/viewall.html.

CONTEXT

The number of faxes or packages we received daily was always different, but whether it was 10 or 100, it was my responsibility to receive each. This meant signing the courier's log, entering the information in our own log, and informing staff that a package or fax had come. The monotony of this responsibility was sometimes welcomed, and sometimes, I detested it. On the days when I was extremely busy, I welcomed the calm this chore brought. On the days when I had next to nothing to do, however, such repetition proved even more irksome.

But whether it was a frantic day or a slow day, it was never a good day when you approached my desk and asked, "Leslie, did a fax come for me?"

DISCUSSION

Of the zillion, annoying questions an assistant is asked each day, this is arguably the king of them all! The level of irritation this simple question triggered would surprise you. The stress I suffered to suppress the impulse to reply, "Did I call you?" to answer instead, "No, Joyce. Nothing has come for you," was unreal. Daily, without fail, you and other staff asked me the following variations of the same question. (Pay special attention to *what I was really thinking*.)

Your Question	My Reply	*But I Was Really Thinking...*
"I'm expecting a package. Can you let me know when it comes?"	"Sure."	*NO! I'm going to let it sit up here and not say anything. Better yet, I'm going to take it home with me.*
"Did I get a fax from Tabatha?"	"No."	*Yeah, but just for the fun of it, I'm going to wait until the end of the day to tell you.*
"Sandra said that she faxed me a copy of my American Express invoice. Have you seen it?"	"No."	*Oh, you mean the one that after it came through I was suddenly overcome with the impulse to throw it in the trash versus tell you about it LIKE I'VE DONE EVERY OTHER TIME?!*
[looking at other received packages on the desk ledge] "Hmm. Mine still hasn't come, huh?"	"No, not yet."	*What are you talking about? Don't you see it? Right there. Yeah, the invisible one!*

On several occasions, your husband met you for lunch and you would ask these comparable questions:

Your Question	My Reply	***But I Was Really Thinking...***
"I'm expecting Jerry about 1:30. Can you let me know when he gets here?"	"Sure."	*NO! I'm going to have him sit out here with me and not say anything. Better yet, I'm going to take him home with me.*
[at 1:35] "Is Jerry here yet?"	"No, not yet."	*What are you talking about? Don't you see him? Right there. Yeah, the invisible man!*

If it was my job to inform you when a package, fax, or visitor had come for you, then you did not need to inquire before I told you. Once, on a day when I was admittedly not in a good mood, you asked me about whether a package had come for you. I ignored you and hurried to shuffle papers on my desk. I hoped you would get the hint and just walk away. Instead, you asked again, at which moment I began coughing and wheezing and gasping for air. I threw my body back and forth violently in my chair, clasping my throat and face, shutting my eyes tightly so that they would begin to tear. Even Jacob looked unsure about whether I really needed help.

After about a minute of this, I jumped up and ran to the bathroom. I swung open the stall door just to make extra noise and sat on the toilet for a good 10 minutes . . . doing absolutely nothing. When I came back to my desk, you were gone, and Jacob was on the floor laughing. I smiled and took my seat again: "If I have to act like that from now on, I swear I'm not gonna answer that question again!"

After he regained his composure, he commented: "What's funny is that she never even went to check on you!" It was my turn to laugh, but I figured you knew I was faking. And I was certain that if I hadn't been clear any other day, I was clear that day: I was SICK of that question!

In jest, and generally during our friendlier conversations, I tried to explain why such a question was unnecessary and annoying. Sometimes you laughed at my impressions of staff, especially the one of Eric looking for his computer deliveries when I had not told him anything had come yet. But clearly, your laughter was not a sign of agreement because you continued to offer the following excuses:

- ✔ **The fax is important.**

Technically, there are not any important or unimportant faxes. When *any* fax came in, I had to call you. Unless a fax came in where I should have (1) dialed your extension faster, (2) paged you over the intercom, (3) jumped up and sprinted it to your office, or (4) folded it into a paper plane and flown it to you, *then it was never important*!

- ✔ **I'm just giving you a heads up that a package is coming—that's all.**

Pray tell, what exactly is a heads up? Did anything that I was required to do change because you gave me a heads up? Didn't I still have to log the package and call the staff for which it had come? Yes, I gathered that it was some type of advance notice, or disguised request for me to be more alert than usual, but if responsibilities and expectations did not change because I had a "heads up," then here's a heads up: YOU'RE ANNOYING ME!

- ✔ **It's just that I have to courier that over to the Hill when it gets here.**

This was another (poor) attempt to deem items "important," so my position was the same: I WILL LET YOU KNOW WHEN IT GETS HERE! I always did. It was my job. It did not matter what you had to do with the package once it arrived. I did not care what the fax was about. I did not care if the president himself was visiting.[6] Whatever and whoever came, however it came, I was going to tell you!

Now, lest I imply you never had a right or obligation to know when something or someone had come—of course, you did. However, if I did not have a habit of leaving visitors in the reception area or neglecting to inform you when faxes came in, and the like, then to ask me about these things was completely aggravating.

In this same vein, there were other questions that were annoying because they were demeaning, and I will say in advance of this discussion that, generally, you were not guilty of this type.

I do not know if you remember when Jacob was out for three weeks following his wife's surgery. I was left without any relief for the restroom, lunch, breaks, etc. Every day, I waited as long as I could before going to the restroom—at least I did that first week. That Tuesday or Wednesday of the second week, Brandy walked past my desk on her way to the front kitchen. I asked her if she could grab the phones for me while I ran to the restroom, and she asked me, "**How long are you going to be?**"

Joyce, was it going to kill her to cover the phones for a few minutes? She did not have any meetings scheduled, and she was only going to the kitchen. Later the same day, around 3:15, I noticed Gordon waiting for the elevator. I had not been informed he was leaving early or that he had any outside meetings. I was only curious because he appeared to be leaving for the day, so I ran out to catch him and asked if he would be returning. Without even turning to face me, he answered, "**Who needs to know?**"

Gordon's response did not surprise me, of course, but it still irritated me. I answered, "I'm sure Joyce would rather me tell callers

[6] This statement is purely for effect because I love my President Obama!

that *'you're gone for the day'* or *'out of the office until such-n-such time.'* But don't worry about it. I'm happy to say, *'The bastard isn't at his desk and didn't want to tell me if he'll be returning. Please hold for his voicemail!'*"

When he finally turned around to face me (and maybe even lunge at me), I gave him the most hate-filled eye roll I could and disappeared through the doors. Joyce, what reason other than work would I have had for inquiring about Gordon's whereabouts? He wasn't my ride home. He didn't owe me money. I didn't care WHERE he was going, and if he didn't come back at all, that would have been fine, too! But his question (and his attitude) demeaned my position and me.

I know how the entire office is affected when the administrative staff is short, especially those who double as receptionists, but is there no one else in the office (besides the support) "good enough" to answer the phones while someone goes to the bathroom for goodness' sake?

Gordon could have said, "No, I'm gone for the day. Please take messages." I know I did not necessarily wait for an answer, but we both know he was not going to give me one, anyway. Thirty minutes later, when you came looking for him and got irritated when I said I did not know where he had gone or if he would be back, now you know why!

Still, other questions were annoying because they were just plain dumb. The king of this type usually happened when you were out of the office and called to speak with someone who happened to be on the phone at the time. "**How long are they going to be?**" Joyce, how in the world could I know that? When you were in the office, did you tell me how long you would be on each of your calls? Then what made you think I would know that about someone else's phone calls?

On occasion, you would walk through the reception area and notice someone sitting and ask, "Have you been helped?" Why would you ask such a dumb question? Had Jacob and I conspired on those days to see how long we could make visitors sit without being greeted and assisted? Even worse, when you learned for whom the visitor was waiting, you sometimes asked us, "Have you let so-n-so know he's here?"

Help me, Holy Ghost!

There is still one question that is arguably the king of all annoying questions, and that is because it is a combination of annoying, demeaning, and just plain dumb: **Are you busy?** If we say no, then we risk appearing like we do not have enough responsibility or work. But worse, we risk appearing lazy and useless, with zero initiative.

Instead of seeking more responsibility or work, we have chosen to sit idle—simply pretending to work. Then, what if we answer, "Yes"? "Yes, I'm busy." *Oh you are, are you? Too busy to hear what I, the boss, have to say to you? Too busy to give me, the boss, five minutes of your precious little time?*

We can't win for losing with this stupid question, so stop asking it! Instead, consider asking, "Do you have a minute?" Or ask: "What are you working on?" Majority of the time, that is all you want to know anyway. You want to know if I have time to hear about something else you would like for me to work on. If you do not approach my desk and find me playing Bejeweled on my phone, then it is safe to assume you already know whether I am busy or not.

COMPROMISE

The following table provides a general guideline to help managers distinguish legitimate questions from annoying questions.

If the question . . .	Then it is likely . . .
Centers on a routine function that an assistant has proven capable of handling without error	☐ **Legitimate** ☒ **Annoying**
Sounds rhetorical in nature	☐ **Legitimate** ☒ **Annoying**
Seems condescending, demeaning, or can provoke anger or agitation	☐ **Legitimate** ☒ **Annoying**
Seems unclear or indirect and could have been asked a variety of alternate ways	☐ **Legitimate** ☒ **Annoying**
If the question . . .	**Then it is likely . . .**
Seeks information that is new, may have changed, or is not commonly known	☒ **Legitimate** ☐ **Annoying**
Reveals information that is new, has changed, or is not commonly known	☒ **Legitimate** ☐ **Annoying**
Seeks confirmation of work performed	☒ **Legitimate** ☐ **Annoying**
Expresses its intent clearly and directly	☒ **Legitimate** ☐ **Annoying**

I have suggested that questions are "likely" annoying or legitimate because I recognize that exceptions exist, including the fact that legitimate questions can become dumb and annoying, as well.

✔ **If the question centers on a routine function that an assistant has proven capable of handling without error, then it is likely annoying.**

To make the request that I let you know when something came for you was annoying because it was what I did anyway. However, there were times when John was working on your computer, and you moved to another space to work. At that point, the request is no longer annoying, but necessary. At that point, you are not telling me to do what I already know to do, but you are telling me to call you *in John's office* if I need to reach you for anything.

The same applies to visitors, as well. You did not have to tell me to let you know when each visitor came because I never left anyone in the reception area. However, when you were leaving the building and were going to be gone when the visitor came, you absolutely needed to say, "Leslie, I am running across the street. If Larissa comes before I get back, can you let Gordon know she's here? He'll take her into the conference room for me."

✔ **If the question seems condescending, demeaning, or can provoke anger, then it is likely annoying.**

It is no one's fault that administrative support is sometimes short, so it is not fair we are the only people inconvenienced when this happens. When I needed relief to use the restroom, for example, and asked others to relieve me, I should not have been asked how long I was going to be. If I mistake that someone is available to take my place for a little while, then he or she should inform me of that.

To say to me, "Well, Leslie, I actually have a meeting with Jack now" or "I can't. I'm late for an appointment and have to leave now," is a much more civil response. I once answered Brandy, "I don't know how long I'll be peeing, Brandy. I'll try to be about five minutes. Make that 10 because I wash my hands with water <u>and</u> soap!" Yes, it was rude and unprofessional, but so was her attitude.

Jacob and I tried to compel you many times to rethink the front-desk relief policy. We worked well at coordinating our lunches, leave, and breaks so that at least one of us was always present. However, on the unplanned occasions when there was only one of us, there was not an organized back-up system in place, and your desire was to have someone at the front desk to answer phones (greet visitors, etc.) at all times. This meant he or I needed to look for someone to sit up front for us to 1) take our two 15-minute breaks (authorized by law); 2) use the restroom (required of all animals); 3) drop off packages to the FedEx drop box (determined by work); and 4) execute other things like take a proper lunch, put away supplies, or run to the vending machine.

I asked you to consider allowing us to leave the desk unattended for quick errands or more important work errands like taking packages to the drop-box. However, you maintained your position that the phones and reception area be "manned" at all times. Jacob and I came to you many times with details of the lack of cooperation from other staff and appealed to you to address it on our behalf. You never did.

- ✔ **If the question seeks confirmation of work completed, then it is likely legitimate.**

Often, you asked me to complete quick, small tasks for you such as making copies of a document, printing a file on special-sized paper, conducting research online, etc. With requests such as these, the deadline was obvious: right away or as soon as possible. Once, you asked me to print a copy of the Sanitation Committee roster for Mr. Greer, who was with you and Gordon in your office finishing a meeting. Minutes later, you walked by my desk on the way to the file room to grab a copy of a publication for him, noticed a document printing and asked me, "Is that the roster?" I told you it was, you waited for it, and then took it with you. That was a legitimate question/assumption.

As mentioned earlier, however, even legitimate questions can become annoying, too. When you concluded some requests with instructions to "let me know when you finish" or "bring it to me when you're done," that changed things. If I have not brought anything to you, then it is likely not done, so to keep asking me if I am finished, when I have not put anything in your hands, is annoying! To make matters worse, for some requests or projects, you gave me a due date. Yet, you continuously asked, "Leslie, what's the status of that report?" THE STATUS IS . . . IT'S NOT DUE YET! GET AWAY FROM ME!

If the priority level changes, then for goodness' sake, communicate *that* to me. If who I give it to when I'm done or what I do with it when finished changes, tell me *that*. But for you to keep inquiring not only implies you do not trust me to complete the project correctly, but it also implies I am behind schedule when I am not. ANNOYING!

SUMMARY

I would bet money that the individual who encouraged people "not to sweat the small stuff" never worked in a support position. He or she does not know how the littlest thing can be so amazingly frustrating, especially when it is endured time and time again. However, that fact alone does not make a "small" thing BIG. Everyone, regardless of position, experiences people and behavior that annoys, and we support employees are not exempt. Things and people will get on our nerves—there is no escaping it—so we have an obligation, as well, to preserve our own mental health by sweating the small stuff a little less.

This is only where annoyances are concerned, however. Employees cannot "grin and bear" incidents that have moved from being annoying to degrading. When something has progressed and now demeans a person or his position, management must step in.

The main area where demeaning behavior often begins is the front desk (i.e., the phones). If an office has a system in place for assistants and receptionists to leave the desk without drama, then they are already mindful of this problem. Even if such a system is in place, employers should also address the attitude that some back-up staff possess, especially when that attitude leads to mistreating the support employee.

Many times—and hopefully it is unbeknownst to management—the staff who fill-in for receptionists and assistants do so quite begrudgingly. They purposely and regularly arrive late to give relief, and may even arrive with an attitude about having to provide relief in the first place; they suddenly disappear moments before their scheduled times; or they conveniently forget a meeting or some other *obligation*, leaving the support employee to find another replacement (in a pool of candidates unwilling to provide back-up in the first place, mind you).

The administrative staff should not have to endure this kind of behavior, and management should not allow it. Managers cannot make people have smiles on their faces or make them feel excited to do a job they do not want to do. However, they can require more cooperative spirits by instituting some kind of reprimand or penalty for uncooperative behavior. The receptionist or other support employee did not write the rules, but whether other employees like it or not, they have to abide by them.

Attachment Four

Unrealistic Expectations

If something is irrational, that means it won't work. It's usually unrealistic.[7]

-Albert Ellis

---

[7] Brainy Quote, "Unrealistic Quotes." Accessed March 24, 2013. www.brainyquote.com/quotes/keywords/unrealistic.html.

CONTEXT

Sometimes I ate lunch in the second break room, at some nearby restaurant, the cafeteria, or—as was my preference—at my desk. During one such lunch, I walked to Subway, came back, and while eating, watched So You Think You Can Dance *on hulu.com. I noticed Gordon approach out of my periphery, and I even noticed when he stopped. But between watching my program and just not caring, I had forgotten about all of it until about ten minutes before I left that day.*

You and Gordon asked if you could have a minute. I glanced at my watch. You chuckled, "I know it's almost time for you to go, but it won't take long."

I pushed my chair back from the desk and gave Jacob a smile as I stood to follow you both into your office.

Gordon spoke first. "First, even though we have not always seen eye to eye, blah blah blah. I think you are an exceptional employee yada yada yada. Since your coming, you have whatever whatever whatever."

I glanced impatiently again at my watch. He sighed.

"Earlier today," he started, "I was coming to give you back the minutes from the board meeting to make some changes, and I noticed you were watching television at your desk. I mean you had ear phones on, your chair was reclined—"

"Gordon, please," I interrupted. "My chair was not reclined."

"Whether it was reclined or not isn't the point—"

"No, it **is** *the point because to say it was reclined when it wasn't is lying."*

"Leslie, I'm not going to do this with you today. I walked out front and noticed you watching television! How do you explain that?"

"I don't have to explain anything!" I snapped. "How come you noticed everything else, but not my food? Did you ***notice*** *the time? I WAS AT LUNCH!"*

"Let's calm down," you sighed and proceeded to rub your temples. Immediately, I felt badly.

I often wondered what you thought of the back and forth between Gordon and me. I knew you had to be sick of us, and I often imagined what you would do when you finally snapped.

"I apologize, Joyce." I said. "I ***was*** *watching television, but I was at lunch. Now, I have eaten lunch at my desk many times, and sometimes, I'm watching movies, paying bills, shopping online . . ."*

"Playing games, checking personal e-mail," Gordon interrupted.

"Gordon, PLEASE!" you jumped up visibly irritated. "Just stop."

I hated Gordon already, but even more at that moment. Running to tattle on me . . . again . . . like a child—waiting for the perfect opportunity to run down his list of my faults and "offenses." I watched your disapproving stare in his direction, and I just knew he was finally about to get his. I smiled. We waited a few more minutes in silence for you to speak again. I was sorely disappointed when you did.

"Gordon, will you give Leslie the copy of the 'Computer Use Policy' for her to reread, and then she can go? Leslie, thank you for staying."

DISCUSSION

As I walked back to my desk to grab my things and leave, I paid attention only to what you (or Gordon) had highlighted:

INTERNET, E-MAIL, AND COMPUTER USE POLICY[8]

Policy Statement

The computer network is the property of Trully & Associates (the Company) and is to be used for legitimate business purposes. Users are provided access to the computer network to assist them in the performance of their jobs. All Users have a responsibility to use the Company's computer resources and the Internet in a professional, lawful and ethical manner. Abuse of the computer network or the Internet, may result in disciplinary action, including possible termination, and civil and/or criminal liability.

Prohibited Activities

Without prior written permission from The Company, The Company's computer network may not be used to disseminate, view or store commercial or personal advertisements, solicitations, promotions, destructive code (e.g., viruses, Trojan horse programs, etc.) or any other unauthorized materials. Occasional limited appropriate personal use of the computer is permitted if such use does not a) interfere with the User's or any other employee's job performance; b) have an undue effect on the computer or company network's performance; or c) violate any other policies, provisions, guidelines or standards of this agreement or any other of the Company. Further, at all times users are responsible for the professional, ethical and lawful use of the computer system. Personal use of the computer is a privilege that may be revoked at any time.

Frivolous Use

Computer resources are not unlimited. Network bandwidth and storage capacity have finite limits, and all Users connected to the network have a responsibility to conserve these resources. As such, Users must not deliber-

[8] Maurice @ RealLinks. "Template for Your Company Internet Usage Policy." Accessed March 27, 2013. http://community.spiceworks.com/how_to/show/2537-template-for-your-company-internet-usage-policy.

ately perform acts that waste computer resources or unfairly monopolize resources to the exclusion of others. These acts include, but are not limited to, sending mass mailings or chain letters, spending excessive amounts of time on the Internet, playing games, engaging in online chat groups or other social media, uploading or downloading large files, accessing streaming audio and/or video files, or otherwise creating unnecessary loads on network traffic associated with non-business-related uses of the Internet.

Needless to say, I went home quite annoyed that evening. To me, you and Gordon missed the most important part of what we had just discussed—**I WAS AT LUNCH!** I realize that it was not immediately recognizable because I was still at my desk, and even if he had noticed my food, he might still assume I was "working" through lunch. Many times, that was exactly what I was doing. If I did not want a full-blown break, I would eat at my desk so I could finish working on something.

Sometimes, however, I expected to take a full lunch at my desk and NOT continue working. On those days, I ate at my desk so I could continue talking to Jacob, play games, check e-mail, etc.[9] Yet, as long as I remained at my desk, I realized that people still had no way of knowing which kind of lunch I was taking. This is why I at least remained amenable to being "interrupted" whenever I ate at my desk.

If Gordon had come to me about the minutes (instead of lurking behind me like some creepy predator), I would have gladly (and kindly, believe it or not) explained that I was at lunch and would revise the minutes as soon as I was done. If he would have then informed me that the task was a priority, I would have paused or shortened my lunch to comply. However, he did not allow the

[9] Sometimes, I ate at my desk because it was easier to have a longer lunch. If I ate at my desk, you had no way of knowing what time my lunch started, so I could always act like I was still within my 60 minutes.

incident to play out that way because the overwhelming point for him, as he later expressed, was that I was watching television, period: "And you can't possibly think that sitting at your desk watching television is appropriate while at work."

Well, clearly, that is exactly what I thought and will now discuss with you the two issues you and Gordon failed to recognize.

Respecting the Lunch Hour (especially the assistant's)

From the moment I walked through the doors in the morning and through them again in the evening, I was at the beck and call of you, Gordon, all of Trully & Associates, its members and clients, visitors—everyone! And contrary to how that sounds, it is not a complaint. It was my job. And I got that part. But as a result of having to tend to everyone else for hours on end, I looked ever the more to the 60 minutes[10] I got each day for lunch. Those 60 minutes were the only time I had to refresh and recharge mentally and physically. It was the <u>only</u> time that was mine alone, so I hated to have it interrupted—least of all for foolishness.

Now again, when I voluntarily chose to share this time with others by eating at my desk, I did not mind interruptions. However, there were other days when I wanted to eat at my desk without being bothered at all—and that desire was not out of line. I did not have the luxury of a door I could close to enjoy my lunch in peace and/or engage in whatever recreational/personal business I wanted to at the time. There are a fortunate few assistants who have this privilege, but the majority of us, and receptionists in particular, must bear the burden of open-space work stations that keep

---

[10] God bless the poor souls who only get 30 minutes. And honestly, who thought of 30 minutes for lunch? By the time I get my food from the refrigerator, warm it up in the microwave, and take it to wherever I am eating, I've already spent 15 minutes. And just forget it if I have to walk to some store or cafeteria to get my food. Thirty minutes for lunch is just madness.

everyone's ears in your conversations and eyes on your computer screen all day long!

While we understand these logistics come with the job, it does not negate the fact that we still have a right to the same privacy that a door automatically affords others. Since we cannot get it any other time of day, we at least deserve it during lunch.

Once, you tried to oblige me by allowing me to hang a "Will Return" clock at my desk. Underneath the clock, I hung my own "Out to Lunch" sign, and you remember that for awhile, this worked. Everyone got a kick out of it, and several people would pretend they couldn't see me sitting at my desk when placing items in my inbox! It all remained cute and did not present a problem until Gordon was removed as my direct supervisor. *Suddenly*, it became an issue.

I remember the evening we walked out together, and you said: "Leslie, I think you should take down the clock and lunch sign. It's a little rude now that I think about it."

eye roll

Give me a break! You know my intent was not to be rude. It was merely the byproduct of not having a door to close, yet still expecting to be granted some semblance of privacy during my lunch hour (even when I chose to eat at my desk). When I mentioned this in a subsequent meeting with you and Gordon, he callously suggested: "That's what the break rooms are for."

I did not even bother to reply because, once again, he missed the whole point. I could have eaten downstairs in the cafeteria or gone outside of the building for lunch, too. The point was that I was entitled to be left alone for 60 minutes every day. Just because I chose to remain in the office during lunch, and at my desk in particular, did not change things. And for his information, eating in the break room is NOT the greatest alternative.

First, who is in the mood to greet and talk to everyone who enters while trying to enjoy your day's only solace? In one hour, Christian filled his water bottle at least three times . . . and he would speak each time he walked into the room! Who does that? He would speak every time he walked by our desk, too. If I have spoken to you once already, I do not have to do it every time I see you. By the third, fourth, or fifth time, you're just being stupid! Christian was a sweet guy, but he made me want to eat at my desk just to avoid him.

And God help me each time Kathleen entered and commented on my lunch. "Uh oh, Leslie, that's the third time this week you've eaten McDonald's," or "Bacon on that grilled chicken sandwich again?" Do you know how obnoxious that was? I know I did not have the greatest eating habits, but what concern was that of hers? She wasn't my doctor! Once, when she noticed me eating a salad, she commented, "Oh gawd, that looks delicious. Good job, Leslie," and then proceeded to e-mail me articles from an online magazine about reclaiming one's life through healthier eating! After the third article, I politely replied: "Kathleen, please stop sending these. I appreciate the gesture, but I am not interested in reading this stuff and am reclaiming my inbox!"

If I wanted to bring a pig in, throw it up on the table and rip into him, it was not her business. Just because I sat in the breakroom (or even at my desk) with my lunch in plain view of everyone did not mean I liked my meals being commented on. Neither did it mean I wanted to be seen eating. I am not an impolite eater, but to have someone "catch" you with your mouth opened wide (eager to receive your food)—or engage you in conversation while eating and have to tell you there is food around your mouth or, God forbid, catch you licking your fingers after a favorite, messy meal—was the worst!

Now, forgive my digression. I know these are pet peeves over which you had no control, but what you could control—and what I asked you to address on my and Jacob's behalf—was *staff interrupting us while at lunch . . . in the break room . . . about work . . . that could wait until we "returned!"*

Again, I cannot and am not complaining about being interrupted when eating at my desk, but if I made it a point to get up, walk away from my desk, and eat somewhere else, why would people still think it was okay to bother me? Now, I am not talking about for true work emergencies,[11] but for things that really could have waited.

Once, Beth came running into the breakroom, almost out of breath, "I went by your desk and Jacob told me you were at lunch. So I went downstairs thinking maybe you were eating in the cafeteria. Then, I went to the break room on the other side, first, didn't see you there, so I came to this one."

Now, I knew I had worked on a spreadsheet for her that morning, but I had finished that before I left for lunch. In fact, I was late leaving for lunch because I stayed to finish it. So immediately, I grew worried I had made a mistake or she had not gotten my e-mail.

"Is everything okay with the spreadsheet?"

---

[11] Food for thought: If I chose to eat lunch outside of the office/building all together, and an "emergency" arose, wouldn't it have to wait until I returned anyway? Or at the very least, wouldn't someone else have to get it done in my absence (See "Other Duties as Assigned")? So are there real work emergencies when someone is at lunch?

"Huh? Oh, no. It looks great. I printed a copy, went to staple it, was out of staples. Went to the supply cabinet to get some more and noticed that we're running low on the purple notepads. And you know my CVB meeting is next week, so I was wondering if you had already ordered some more."

crickets

I was beyond incensed. She walked all over the building to interrupt me at lunch behind notepads! Never mind they were not needed for another week.

Reasonable Office Behavior

Closely related to respecting the assistant's lunchtime is recognizing *reasonable* office behavior during and outside of lunchtime. The reason this is an issue is because management mistakenly assumes employees will not (or should not) conduct or engage in personal business or activities during work hours.

Uhhhh . . . !

Support staff, like managers and other senior level staff, have the right to do whatever is reasonable during the day. If we want to go pay a bill, drop off dry cleaning, go get a shoe fixed, or run some other quick errand, we can. If we want to make a doctor, dentist, or hair appointment, go to the appointment, and then return to work—we can. If we want to shop online, instant message friends, listen to music (with our earphones plugged in or with the computer speakers at a respectful level), we can. We can even sit at our desks and watch a movie or television online if we want to!

I know you remember the reaction from Gordon the day he found Melvin, Victor, Carl, Everett, Cecilia, and me in the break room at lunch playing cards. The following Monday at the staff meeting, he spent a good 30 minutes talking about a "sight [he'd] never ever witnessed before, in all [his] 39 years of work." You would have thought he found us shooting craps the way he carried on. It was UNO® for goodness' sake! Sometimes, people would come in and watch us play, and once or twice, Sara Ann, the most uptight chief financial officer any office has ever known, joined us. She had as good a time as we did laughing, talking, and just hanging out.

Now, I would think that because we reserved such an activity for lunch, there would not be a problem. We had not taken a longer lunch than was allowed. We never had a noise complaint made. We were not even using the only area staff had to eat because there were two break rooms. It was not until our meeting that I finally realized Gordon's issue was not that it was during lunch, but that it was done period. He took issue with *any* non-business activity during business hours.

Who expects employees to work eight, nine, or more hours a day without ever engaging in non-work-related activities? What parent will never make or receive a call from a child's daycare or school? Find me the husband or wife who will never e-mail each other about dinner, a movie, an upcoming trip, weekend plans, the children, or some other personal subject—and I mean from Yahoo, Gmail, Hotmail or some other personal account. Show me an employee who has never been online to update a Facebook status, send some meaningless tweet, order clothes, browse TMZ website, or the like.

Many times, during our staff meetings—the good ones, anyway—we discussed certain videos and happenings in the world. I remember the staff meeting after Michael Jackson's death; we remained in the conference room for a good 30 or 40 minutes discussing all of the chaos and theories. Where do you think we watched some of the coverage? AT WORK!

Gordon's grandstanding always surprised me because I know he was aware that we knew he made personal phone calls, sent personal e-mails, ran personal errands, etc., too! I personally delivered to him a copy of his Expedia confirmation for his Punta Cana trip last summer. I had gone to the printer to pick up my own job, noticed it, and took it to him in his office. Instead of saying thank you, he took five minutes at the next staff meeting to talk about people picking up other people's faxes and documents: "They could contain sensitive or confidential information, so let us concern ourselves with our own documents."

*deep breath*

I won't know a document is or is not mine unless I look at it, right? Now, if I noticed it wasn't mine, but then continued reading, then you can rightly take issue with that. However, if something is sensitive, it should not be sent to the main printer in the first place! It should be sent to a desktop printer (which he had). If he accidentally sent the personal document to the network printer by mistake (or on purpose so it could print in color), he should have gone immediately to the printer to grab it like I do when I print personal documents.

I recall when Gordon even caught an attitude with you when you inquired how his wife was doing. "What do you mean?" he asked, his eyebrows raised.

"Oh," you hesitated. "She fell down the stairs in your home last weekend, didn't she?"

"She's fine," he grumbled, turned his back to you, and walked away.

I do not know what his problem was. The entire office knew because we heard his conversations with her drunk butt! When he wasn't on the phone in his office, he would step out into the hallway to use his cell phone . . . where the acoustics made his voice even louder!

Whether people pretended they never conducted personal business during office hours or never used company or other equipment for these personal matters—attempting to hide they were doing it or choosing always to do it during their lunch hour—the fact is that *everyone,* including management, used company time for personal business. For an employer to expect that people should not, is unreaslitic.

COMPROMISE

I don't think you disagree that brief and occasional personal use of the electronic mail system or the Internet—and I will add phone—is acceptable. In fact, our policy states that "occasional limited appropriate personal use of the computer is permitted..." The key words in this policy are that such use must be *limited* and *appropriate*, which is the first layer of consideration surrounding this issue.

I am fully aware there are certain behaviors and "uses" of the computer and phone system that are *universally* inappropriate or excessive. Our policy offers a number of them,[12] and I would never argue that employers should make these behaviors allowable. However, as "inappropriate" or "excessive" as some standards are, they are still difficult to enforce because gray areas exist.

Do I think that on a slow day or during my lunch I should be allowed to watch a movie, listen to online radio stations, get on Facebook, play a game, instant message, and the like? Most definitely. However, I recognize the danger inherent in allowing employees to download even suitable movies or games from certain sites because of potential viruses, consumption of bandwidth, and unwanted access to computer systems and data. Even though these activities are not excessive or inappropriate, employers still cannot allow unrestricted access to do these kinds of things.

Is the employee who sits on the company phone (or personal cell phone, for that matter) carrying on long, loud personal conversa-

---

[12] The following behaviors are universally inappropriate, and for the most part, no exceptions exist: sending, receiving, or accessing pornographic materials; using abusive, profane, threatening, racist, sexist, or otherwise objectionable language in either public or private messages; causing congestion, disruption, disablement, alteration, or impairment of Company networks or systems (one exception is causing network, system, or computer congestion from downloading a work-related file, which can happen).

tions all day long wrong? Absolutely, but what if that same employee still completes his or her assignments—outstandingly, mind you—and is regularly commended for exemplary work in his department?

Justin took at least ten smoke breaks in eight hours, was always "sick" on Fridays and/or Mondays, and never took a lunch shorter than an hour and a half. Yet, he was never late to a meeting; he was organized; his presentations were incredible; and he stayed on top of his work to the point of several commendations by you *and* the board of directors!

Excessive is defined as "beyond what is considered acceptable, proper, usual, or necessary,"[13] and certainly, that is what some of Justin's behavior was. However, as an employer, you would be remiss if you did not still acknowledge that his work and contribution to the organization are stellar. It is because of these "gray" areas that employers should additionally consider whether the activity or behavior "interfere[s] with [an employee] or other employee's job performance . . ."

What work had I neglected to complete by watching television at my desk? Even if we ignore for a moment the fact that I was at lunch, what assignment had I completed incorrectly? To whom had I failed to respond?

Last year, before I left on maternity leave, I ordered some items for my son's nursery and had them delivered to me at work. When the order arrived, I was excited—of course. After I opened everything, I noticed one of his wooden letters was the wrong color. No, it was not an emergency (or even work-related), but I knew the call would not last very long. So I called customer service.

---

[13] Microsoft Word Reference Books. "Excessive." Accessed March 24, 2013.

Brandy happened to come by, escorting some people to the door with whom she had just finished a small meeting. I knew they could hear my conversation, not because I was loud, because they were standing right in front of my desk. When they first came out, I had been on hold. Shortly thereafter, the representative returned to the phone, and I continued my business with her. Seconds later, Brandy approached my desk to ask if I could quickly print out a copy of the board of directors' calendar.

All assistants have to be able to multi-task, and I am no exception. Even though I was on the phone, I acknowledged with a nod that I heard her and proceeded to find the calendar, all while still talking to customer service. I was in the middle of responding to the representative when Brandy whispered, "Make it three copies, Leslie." I heard her the second time and nodded again, but I also put my finger up. I needed her to be quiet so I could hear what the agent was saying.

No surprise, Brandy did NOT appreciate that. She turned back to the gentlemen, excused herself, and then stormed off. I finished my call, printed the copies, and distributed them to the men in the waiting area. When she returned with copies of the calendar, the gentlemen politely explained that I had given them a copy already. She smiled, "Oh, great!" They exchanged their final goodbyes, and she stormed by my desk, again . . . and promptly marched into Gordon's office to tell her version of the events.

Of course, her version had all of the boxes and items strewn across my desk, the desk ledge, and even Jacob's side of the desk (who was out that day). I was talking loudly on the phone and rude to her when she approached me about printing the calendars. You told me you knew Brandy was exaggerating, yet you still asked me to be a little more mindful of when I made personal phone calls.

Why?

Did making that call at that moment interfere with my job function, responsivness, or ability to complete the task I had been given? Truthfully, at that moment, Brandy was disturbing me. I was on that call before her work need arose, so I had not made a personal call at an inappropriate time. I was legitimately busy when she needed me—personal call or not—so she should have waited for me to finish, or made the copies herself like she subsequently did. In hindsight, I probably should not have raised my finger, but that was reflex. I did not do it rudely to embarrass her.

My ability to respond to and perform my duties satisfactorily is all that should have mattered. The day I called PoshTots customer service about my son's order was no exception: my workload had eased for that moment; the front reception area was quiet; and I had not anticipated being long. So I made the call. I could not forsee Brandy would suddenly need me to do something, but that did not make my making a personal call then "wrong."

It just as easily could have been a legitimate business call. Then, what would the difference have been? The fact is that some staff acted as if we were never supposed to be on the phone if it was not business-related: PERIOD. Often, when people approached the desk for Jacob or me and heard we were on a personal call, they would whisper that they would come back. When Gordon approached, however, he heard the personal conversation and just stood there.

Jacob got such a kick out of his pacing back and forth—or watching him walk away and then come right back—as if that would make us hurry because we knew he was waiting. I, on the other hand, was never amused. I hated being rushed off the phone or made to feel like a slacker because I was on the phone in the first place. Once, when he tried to just stand there, I politely put my hand over the receiver and whispered to him that I would come see him when I was done. If I had to caption his expression—well, let's just say it was not friendly, but I did not care. I had the right to call my doctor's office and talk about my fibroids privately, without him listening in or rushing me. Wouldn't you agree?

SUMMARY

I was unaware until recently that giving rest or meal breaks is not a requirement under Federal labor laws.[14] According to the United States Department of Labor, in 2010, there were only 21 states that had laws with some sort of meal period requirements for adult employees. Of the 21, only 7 had separate provisions for rest periods, as well.[15] I think this is absurd, though I would imagine most employers do agree that lunch breaks are necessary. If nothing else, they provide an opportunity for employees to de-stress, replenish, and unwind. Without this time, employees are less likely to be productive or efficient workers.

Do not mistake this issue to be about lunch, however. Sometimes, unwinding and de-stressing does not involve a meal, only. Sometimes, it involves taking care of personal business/errands, playing a game, watching a movie, listening to music, checking e-mail, etc. The time used to partake in these things should *at a minimum* be during lunch, but this is not to say they should not be done outside of lunch. It is highly unrealistic for employers to expect employees to abstain from personal or recreational activities all day long. Aside from the fact that managers engage in the same behaviors, two more realistic considerations are 1) whether the behavior is

---

[14] There are no federal and few state laws requiring employers to even give bathroom breaks, but the Federal Occupational Safety & Health Administration (OSHA) emphasizes that it "requires employers to make toilet facilities available so that employees can use them when they need to do so. The employer may not impose unreasonable restrictions on employee use of the facilities." Occupational Safety and Health Administration, "United State Department of Labor: Interpretation of 29 CFR 1910.141(c)(1)(i): Toilet Facilities." Accessed March 27, 2013. http://www.osha.gov/pls/oshaweb/owadisp.show_document?p_id=22932&p_table=INTERPRETATIONS; EmployeeIssues.Com, "Work Breaks and Meals." Accessed February 4, 2011. http://www.employeeissues.com/breaks_meals.htm.

[15] United States Department of Labor, "Minimum Length of Meal Period Required Under State Law For Adult Employees in Private Sector 1 January 1, 2010." Accessed February 11, 2011. http://www.dol.gov/whd/state/meal2010.htm.

excessive or inappropriate and 2) whether it impedes work performance.

For many things, such as a personal phone call or a quick game of Mahjong, there may never be a perfect time. That is, neither manager nor employee will mutually agree when and whether such things should take place. However, both sides ought to agree that no pass can be given to the employee when work obligations are missed or performance becomes less exemplary. This disrupts and affects an entire office. It should never be tolerated by management, and *no employee*—administrative or otherwise—should expect to get away with it.

Talking on the phone for non-business-related reasons is not a problem. Listening to music on the office computer is not a problem. Playing a game is not a problem. Thirty-minute personal calls where everyone can hear you, however, *are* a problem. Leaving visitors in the reception area while you try to beat your last high score in a game is a problem. Forgetting meetings and being unprepared for them because you are tweeting celebrities and updating Facebook statuses is a problem. You not getting the point of this topic by now is a problem.

Attachment Five

Other *Duties* as Assigned

Executive ability is deciding quickly and getting somebody else to do the work.[16]

- John G. Pollard

[16] The Quote Garden, "Job-related Quotations." Accessed March 24, 2013. http://www.quotegarden.com/jobs.html.

CONTEXT

The incident for this grievance is provided in the following e-mail exchange between Brandy, Maggie, and me. (I assume you know to read from the bottom up):

From: Adams, Brandy [maito:adams.brandy@trullyandassociates.org]
Sent: Wednesday, February 6, 2008 10:33 AM
To: Lewis, Leslie <TRULLYANDASSOCIATES>
Subject: FW: Teleconference

Leslie – is there a maximum number of lines they will be able to add? Also, one of the participants is out of the country. Can they give us a toll-free number so he does not have to make an international call?

From: Jones, Maggie [mailto:jones.maggie@ostproperties.com]
Sent: Tuesday, February 5, 2008 10:13 AM
To: Lewis, Leslie <TRULLYANDASSOCIATES>
Cc: Adams, Brandy <TRULLYANDASSOCIATES>
Subject: FW: Teleconference

We can add lines up to one hour before your call begins. After that, there is a charge of $0.25 per added line.

Regards,
Maggie Jones
Conference Call Operator / OST Properties

From: Lewis, Leslie [mailto:lewis.leslie@trullyandassociates.org]
Sent: Wednesday, February 6, 2008 10:07 AM
To: 'Jones, Maggie'
Cc: Adams, Brandy <TRULLYANDASSOCIATES>
Subject: FW: Teleconference

Maggie, thanks for the number and info. The number of participants may increase—to what, we don't know. When is the latest you will be able to add additional lines for us?

(Please keep Brandy copied on your reply. Thanks.)

From: Adams, Brandy [mailto:adams.brandy@trullyandassociates.org]
Sent: Wednesday, February 6, 2008 9:57 AM
To: Lewis, Leslie <TRULLYANDASSOCIATES>
Subject: FW: Teleconference

Leslie – thanks. I forgot to include a few people on the original invite. RSVPs are still coming in, so it is likely this number will increase. Can you find out how late we can have the number of lines changed before the start time?

From: Lewis, Leslie [mailto:lewis.leslie@trullyandassociates.org]
Sent: Wednesday, February 6, 2008 9:53 AM
To: Adams, Brandy <TRULLYANDASSOCIATES>
Subject: FW: Teleconference

Brandy, below is your dial-in information and pass code for next week's conference call.

From: Jones, Maggie [mailto:jones.maggie@ostproperties.com]
Sent: Tuesday, February 5, 2008 5:16 PM
To: Lewis, Leslie <TRULLYANDASSOCIATES>
Subject: Teleconference

I have set up a conference bridge for February 13, 2008 from 2-2:30 for 15 lines, as requested.

Originator: Brandy Adams (TAA104-2)
Call-in number: 202-555-2690
Pass code: 4849

If you have any questions feel free to contact me via e-mail or phone.

Regards,
Maggie Jones
Conference Call Operator / OST Properties

DISCUSSION

I am sure you remember this incident because it led to a written reprimand in my file. My next reply to Brandy was prompt and short: "Call Maggie and ask her your damn self!!"

Often, Brandy needed me to set-up conference calls for her, and the process was simple: e-mail the property management's office with the details of the call. An e-mail was generated by them and sent to me with the particulars, and then, I forwarded it to her (or whoever the requestor had been).

Though the process usually remained simple like this, there were times when the number of participants changed, the start and end time moved, the date changed, etc. I expressed to you privately, and to everyone else during staff meetings, that in those cases it made more sense for staff to contact the property manager's office directly. Aside from the fact that I hated having to bother someone a million times, a middleman just made no sense.

Who but the people needing the call, special meeting set-up, or other arrangements could articulate their special needs (and changes to those needs)? It was hugely annoying to have me ask the contact a question, have that person ask a follow-up question, and then have to go back to the staff member to get the answer . . . and then report it back to the contact! Or, as in this case, report information to a staff member, and instead of that staff member getting additional information from the source themselves, she looks for me to go back to the source, ask the question, get the answer, report it back to her, get asked another question, and then go back to the source. Brandy knew all of the particulars she required for her call, so why shouldn't *she* have been the one to go back and forth with Maggie?

It was the same when Gordon's computer kept freezing. Any normal person would have just picked up the phone and called the Help Desk. Who better than Gordon could explain what the issue was with *his* computer? Instead, he marched right up to Jacob, and the following conversation was held:

Gordon: "Jacob, I need you to call the Help Desk. Every time I open Word, my computer starts running slow and then freezes, and I have to keep restarting."

Jacob: "Okay."

Me: "OMG! He is a trip!"

Jacob: "I know. It would have taken him how long to call himself?"

Me: "I know!"

Jacob: *(sighs)*

Me: "Put it on speakerphone!"

Jacob: *(laughs)* "No, nosey! You're always looking for trouble." *(I laugh and he dials)*

Help Desk: "Thank you for calling Support. My name is Miguel, and I would love to assist you today. How may I help you?"

Jacob: "Hi, Miguel. My name is Jacob, and I'm calling from Trully and Associates. I have a computer that freezes and runs slow when Microsoft Word is opened."

Miguel: "Okay, I'm sorry to hear that, Jacob. I'd be happy to help you. There's a white sticker on the bottom of your laptop, Jacob. Can you give me that serial number, please?"

Jacob: *(hesitates)* "Oh, I'm sorry. It's not my computer. It's my manager's. Do you mind holding so I can go get that number for you?"

Miguel: "Sure, no problem."

Jacob: *(returns a few minutes later)* "Miguel?"

Miguel: "Yes. I'm still here."

Jacob: "Thanks. That number is 100054803."

Miguel: "Thank you, Jacob. Okay, I see that they have a Dell Vostro 460. Do you happen to know what version of Word is installed on this computer?"

Jacob: "Uhh, no, I don't. Some of us have 0-10 and some of us still have 08. Hold on again, and I'll go find out."

Miguel: "No, don't worry about it. I might be able to do this anyway. Now, is the mouse still able to move or is everything completely frozen?"

By now, I am laughing hysterically, and Jacob is doing everything he can not to lose his composure.

Jacob: "I'm sorry, Miguel. I don't know. Like I said, it's my boss' computer. He could probably tell you better than I can what exactly is happening, how long it's been happening, and all of that. I'm just trying to generate the ticket."

Miguel: "No, problem, Jacob. I understand. Is there any way I can speak with your boss, though, because we may be able to troubleshoot his machine right now without having to send somebody over there?"

I am sure Miguel was even thinking, *Why the heck didn't your boss call then!* It made absolutely no sense for Jacob to call the Help Desk about Gordon's computer when he was likely going to be asked questions he could not answer. Fortunately, Miguel was cool about it, but many times, Jacob and I would become the innocent recipients of harsh retorts, irritated sighs, etc. Even though we did not like it, we certainly understood it.

When you, Brandy, and I met about her incident, in particular, she commented that she felt I was out of line. Her exact comment was, "Leslie didn't want to do her *job*." This conceited thinking is what lies at the root of this issue.

Brandy had this committee conference call every other week, and she wasn't any more organized than she was. She had to piecemeal her needs and questions to me because she did not have a proper gauge on her committee activity. My job was not for her disorganization to annoy me and, in turn, annoy Maggie, too. My *job* was to support the staff, not be taken advantage of because I *was* the support.

This issue manifested in other responsibilities, too. When did it become Jacob's or my job to make copies? Of course, I'm not talking about copying handouts and materials for a meeting. That was our job, absolutely, but do you remember the final straw for Gordon and me? He printed a three-page attachment from an e-mail to his desktop printer, and then brought it to me to make two more copies. When I asked him why he did not just print three copies in his office, we ended up in our final fight. I was pregnant with my second child and definitely needed my job, but I would have whooped him like I was in a street brawl and gladly lost my job that day! His request was absolutely out of line!

If managers could put their egos aside just for a moment, they may be persuaded on my viewpoint. The time it took him to open the attachment, hit print, wait for the document, and then walk it from his office out to my desk, two more copies could have been printed. Then maybe, just maybe, our working relationship may have stood a chance. (Being sarcastic!)

I realize I am not exactly preaching to the choir considering the number of times you brought me something to copy and then return to you. Never mind that it was a one-page document sometimes or that you had to walk pass the copier machine to bring it to me. This is just dumb, Joyce! Honestly.

There were only three people in our entire office who always made their own copies. As much as Jacob and I appreciated this, even they lost all cool points when they left the machine to walk down the hall to tell us that more paper was needed. Just once I wanted to say, "Well, bend your ass down and put some more in it!"

You mean that in an office of executive directors, chief financial officers, project managers, and the like, no one but the administrative assistants can fill a paper tray? Was it that it was our job to do it or that everyone else was too good to do it? As cool as Sandra was, her theatrics were especially hilarious. She would pretend there was something wrong with the machine and ask Jacob or me to take a look. It did not take long to figure out the issue, especially with the blinking TRAY 1 LOAD PAPER error message!

"Oh, was that all," she would chuckle, and then stand aside so we could grab another ream of paper from the shelf (behind the machine).

Sandra was not a stupid woman. She knew good and well what was wrong with the copier, but apparently, program managers did not have to "stoop so low" as to load paper. If she could not find one of us, she still refused to do it. Instead, she would walk to another copier and make her copies there. Forget that in the time it took her to walk to another copier, she could have grabbed some more paper, loaded the machine, and been finished. On top of that, if the machine ran out of paper in the middle of copying, she would manually open the machine and remove her originals from the feeder and glass, creating an even bigger jam for the next user! Once, all four copiers were jammed and displaying a similar error message. Everyone knew who had done it.

Below is an email from you:

From: Trully, Joyce [mailto:trully.joyce@trullyandassociates.org]
Sent: Tuesday, July 15, 2008 12:17 PM
To: Lewis, Leslie <TRULLYANDASSOCIATES>
Subject: SDF Masters Contact

Leslie—can you please add this lady to my contacts?

Dr. Elyssa M. O'Brien
Senior Accounts Executive
SDF Masters, Incorporated
3400 M Street, NE
Rockville, MD 20135

Joyce M. Trully

YOU HAD JUST TYPED THE SAME INFORMATION YOU WANTED ME TO TYPE INTO YOUR ADDRESS BOOK! Seriously! Am I missing something, or was this the laziest, most asinine behavior imaginable? Again, I understood completely what my position/title was, but tell me how this made any sense to you. Why couldn't *you* have opened your Contacts folder and typed this single contact there? It would have taken you all of two minutes. Yes, you are the CEO and I the assistant, but you really thought I had time for that foolishness? Couldn't a request like this be considered abusive on some level?

Prior to this e-mail, you had just forwarded me another e-mail with a presentation attached that you wanted me to print. You sent both of these "requests" shortly after I left for lunch, so I did not even see them until an hour later when I returned. In that time, as Jacob later briefed me, you came looking for me to get the presentation.

"Oh, where is she?" you asked him.

"Lunch. She went early today because I had some work to finish."

"Okay, thanks." You left, and he thought everything was all right until you reappeared a few minutes later. "Do you know where she's eating?"

"No."

"Okay, well, could you have her to come see me as soon as she returns, please?"

When I did return and popped my head into your office, before you even mentioned the e-mail with the presentation, you said, "I checked both break rooms and didn't see you. I even went downstairs to see if maybe you were eating in the cafeteria today."

Annoyed. "Oh, no, my husband was off today, so he met me for lunch. I wasn't in the building at all."

Now, *you* looked annoyed. "Oh, okay. I've seen you eat in the break room before, though, or even at your desk."

"Yes, you have. And I do. But I didn't today."

Lord, have mercy!

Without revisiting the previous grievance, since when was I required to remain in the building or in our suite for lunch? I guess it was your turn that day to disturb my lunch for some dumbness. Just because you happened to be looking for me at that moment did not suddenly make my absence for my rightful lunch hour an inconvenience. Now, let's talk about why you were looking for me in the first place: TO PRINT AN ATTACHMENT FROM AN E-MAIL THAT YOU FORWARDED TO ME! The e-mail and attachment were in *your* inbox. You could have opened both, hit 🖶, and gone on your merry little way.

Suppose I hadn't returned from lunch? Suppose I had choked to death on my food? That presentation would have still gotten printed, right? Just last month, all of the handouts for a board meeting had been prepared by an outside office. In total, there were about 20 attachments. Expecting me to print those was more realistic. I logged into your e-mail from my desk and printed and copied those attachments for your personal notebook. Happily. Without complaint. Because THAT was my job.

COMPROMISE

There is a GROSS misconception about what the support person's "job" is. One of the reasons for this is the notion that certain responsibilities are beneath certain positions. The main reason for this grievance, however, is the careless application of an even more careless phrase: "other duties as assigned."

Now, despite what I have already said about this issue, I do recognize that such an all-inclusive phrase *is* necessary. There are times when tasks and responsibilities must be reassigned due to staff being out sick, on maternity leave, on travel, in training, etc. Also, management must use language that promotes flexibility in a person's position.[17] Using such language gives employees room to grow and advance in their jobs, but the intent of this caveat is frequently misapplied. And when it is, it is a very slippery slope to abusing employees, primarily those in the support position.

Management can begin to address this issue by first looking at our title. The word assist is defined: "to help someone to do or accomplish something."[18] It follows, then, that the job of an administrative assistant is to help someone do or accomplish an administrative task. Implied in our title, however, is the fact that *people must already be doing something* if we are to assist them! We cannot do our jobs if others are not already doing theirs.

Someone must already be trying to change the toner and fail, before my *assistance* is required. You must already be attempting to print something and get pulled away on something else . . . before calling me to finish the printing. Ninety percent of the work we perform involves supporting the work, projects, etc. that someone

---

[17] Smith, Sarah E. 1999. "Letter Perfect: the Ins and Outs of Writing Job Descriptions." *Restaurants USA.* Accessed March 9, 2011. http://dev.restaurant.org/rusa/magArticle.cfm?ArticleID=754.

[18] Microsoft Word Reference Books. "Assist." Accessed March 24, 2013.

else is (already) doing. It has been said that "God helps those who help themselves."[19] Well, so do administrative assistants! Everything we can do, you can do it, too! This is not to assert that support people are useless, but what can be added to that expression is, "Everything we can do, you can do it, too—*and sometimes you should*!"

It is time for management to admit that sometimes what gets "assigned" to support employees are not things that staff need assistance with, but things other people just do not want to do—or feel they are too important to do. As long as *these* things are labeled the support person's "job," the relationship between management and support will continue to be strained.

In the case of Brandy, my job was to assist her with preparations for her committee conference call, and I had done that. The stupid back and forth she was expecting me to do was excessive, and she was only requiring it because she did not want to do it. This was a special case, and she should have been the one to speak with Maggie. Instead, she opted to be lazy.

A more mindful employee would have said, "I know better what's going on with my activity than you do. I'll contact Maggie myself." And may have even added, "Thank you for getting me started." Instead, she said, "I just didn't have time to contact Maggie." Well, what was the difference between the time she *didn't* have to contact Maggie herself and the time she had to keep contacting me with e-mails and questions for Maggie? Come on now! A more truthful statement would have been that she did not *want* to contact Maggie. And that's fine, but do not then say that I was not doing my "job."

---

[19] Sidney, Algernon. "Algernon Sidney: Discourses Concerning Government." The Online Library of Liberty. Accessed March 25, 2013. http://oll.libertyfund.org/index.php?option=com_staticxt&staticfile=show.php?title=223&layout=html.

It was the same thing with Sandra. She was not the only person in the office who refused to put paper in the copier or attempt to change the toner. Obviously, she believed this kind of task was below her pay grade. And you know what? That's fine, too. My self-esteem is still okay. However, to create a jam in the copier and never try to clear it, but instead walk to another copier and leave the error for someone else to fix, is not about how much a person earns. It is just arrogance.

The day she jammed all of the machines, she approached Jacob and me to fix them. I did not even look at her when I spoke: "What did the prompts say?"

"What prompts?" she asked indignant.

She knew damn well what prompts I was talking about, but I was ready to play that day, too. "Oh," I started still looking at my screen, "you need to click the status button on the screen. It'll tell you what's wrong and walk you through how to fix it. It shows you pictures and everything so you should be okay."

I wanted to look up to catch her expression, but I already knew what her face would reveal. Was I being a jerk? Absolutely. But so was she. Looking at the prompts and diagrams on the machine is all Jacob or I would have done, too. We did not have a special touch or magic wand. If we could follow illustrated prompts on the screen, then so could she, especially since *she* jammed the machines in the first place. If she had tried to follow the prompts and couldn't, *then* I would have gladly *assist*ed her.

When she turned to walk away, Jacob gave me one of his *just let it go* looks, and I almost did because, again, Sandra was cool with me. However, when she mumbled while walking away, "Isn't that what you get paid to do?" she lost all cool points. I called out to her, "No, it's not. That's why I'm still sitting here, and you don't have your copies!" And that was the truth. It was not what I was paid to do. It was what people wanted me to feel obligated to do because they felt too good to do it themselves!

How is it that only the admin assistant is expected to refill paper in a copier that the entire office uses all day long? If it runs out while you're copying, just fill the damn thing! How do you justify leaving the machine to come find Jacob or me so we have to come and do what you could have already done? Believe me, I know this sounds arrogant since, again, I was the support employee, but why isn't it arrogant on your part also?

When Jacob transferred Miguel to Gordon so he could speak directly with him about troubleshooting his computer, Gordon was very upset. He put Miguel on hold to buzz Jacob to say that he didn't have time to talk to Help Desk and that it was Jacob's job to handle that for him. I was so proud when Jacob told him, "Then you don't have time to get your computer fixed, Gordon, because I cannot answer the questions he is asking me. He even said he might be able to fix your computer while on the phone. That's why I transferred him to you."

I recall another incident with Jacob and Gordon. Not that long ago, Jacob had one of those busy days when he had a lot of committee meetings to support on the same day—three, to be exact. The first meeting had just ended in conference room 8. The second meeting was an hour later, in the same room *and* during the same time as the third meeting (in rooms A and B). He had hoped to set up the smaller meeting first, but when he got there, he noticed members were still clearing out and lollygagging. So he went downstairs to rooms A and B to set up.

There was a little more expected for the larger meeting, but nothing he was not capable of handling. About 30 minutes before

Gordon's meeting in room 8, he came flying through the doors looking for Jacob.

"Where is he? My people have started to arrive."

Annoyed, I responded dryly. "He's downstairs setting up for your and Tomlyne's meeting."

"No, he isn't. I just came from the room, and he's not there."

Even more annoyed. "If he isn't in your room, then he's probably in the other one. I just said he's setting up for two meetings. Plus, I saw him take down your handouts."

"I know. They're in a chair in the room already, but Tomlyne's group left a few plates and napkins on the table down there. And one of them spilled some water or something, too."

Wait a minute. Let me get this straight. He was hunting down Jacob, at a time when he was completely swamped, to wipe off a table and throw away trash? *What was wrong with his hands*? Honestly! If Sandra's comment did not strike you as arrogant, you cannot ignore the enormous ego behind behavior like this.

Yes, Gordon was the freaking vice president, but since when is anyone too good to throw away trash? Why was he waiting for the administrative assistant to do it? Jacob had his handouts and materials there in the conference room. He did not require a phone, audio, video, or any other set up. All Gordon had to do was clean off the table, put the handouts and sign-in sheet out, and keep it moving! Instead, he acted like Jacob was slacking and leaving him hanging right before his meeting.

I could not wait for Jacob to return so I could tell him, but he returned eager to tell me all about how Gordon waltzed into the other conference room and, *in front of the members who had already arrived for Tomlyne's meeting,* told him to stop what he was doing and come remove the trash from the table in his room and set out his handouts.

As soon as Gordon's meeting was finished, he called Jacob into his office for a "quick meeting." When Jacob returned, he told me that Gordon had given him another copy of his position description, and he showed me where Gordon had highlighted "other duties as assigned." What stood out to me most, however, was the fact he also highlighted a line about maintaining a professional image.

"Why did he highlight 'project a professional company image'?" I asked.

"Because I rolled my eyes, and he told me that wasn't the kind of professional image I should be portraying at work and in front of members."[20]

—

Now, if Jacob or I had never wiped off a table, picked up trash, pushed chairs back under a table, wiped off a dry-erase board, and other menial tasks like this after a meeting, I would understand Gordon's issue. If we had never gone into the break rooms and wiped down the counters or cleaned out the filthy microwaves, refrigerators, and freezers because no one else bothered or cared to do it, then I would empathize. But we did these things. On many occasions. And not because this was our job. These kinds of things had nothing to do with providing administrative support. They were the kinds of things managers and non-support staff could impose on us in the unrighteous and unholy name of "other duties as assigned."

---

[20] But yelling at staff in front of members and guests is?

Understand that any "other duties" assigned to an employee should at least "be reasonably related to the employee's position and qualifications."[21] I understand why people come to the assistant when a copier is out of paper or toner, but sometimes, many times, we performed these duties because it was the polite thing to do. We picked up trash because we already had to go into that room to retrieve equipment, maybe, or set up for another meeting. We wiped the microwave because we were going to use it, anyway.

But guess what? Other people used the copier machines and microwaves, too. So *other duties,* such as replacing toner, cleaning, and the like, could rightly be "assigned" to others, as well. Yet people expected only the support to fulfill these kinds of duties just because we are the support, and that is wrong. It is arrogant, and it needs to end.

Should I be responsible to sort the mail and distribute it? Absolutely, but regularly, you brought me something for someone else in the office or building and expected me to walk it to him or her. Why was that only *my* "other duty" and not yours? Your feet were never broken in the two years I was employed here. If you could walk the envelope or piece of paper to me, then you could walk it to whomever it was going to, right?

I always found it funny that you called yourself assisting *me* by already having the item in an envelope, sealed, with the recipient's name legible (unlike your usual chicken scratch). As if I should have been grateful that I didn't have to guess where it was going. Well, just so you know, I would have been more grateful if you would have delivered it yourself!

---

[21] Smith, "Letter Perfect."

I remember one evening when you caught me just as I was leaving and asked me to put the document you handed me in an envelope and take it to IOP's office on the third floor: "I need this to get to Roberto right away. You can drop it off on your way down to the lobby."

Yeah, I could have, but you could have taken it to him, too—especially since you saw that I was leaving for the day. You had all day long to get that document to me and/or get it to him yourself! As soon as you were out of sight, I threw it into an intra-office envelope and threw that thing right in the pile with the other items being picked up the next morning by the building mailman. I don't know when it was eventually delivered—I assume some time the next day—but whenever it was, it was good enough that you didn't have to ask me about it again. So did it even have to be hand-delivered in the first place? Let alone by *me*?

SUMMARY

Assigning other duties is necessary in any office, but the duties being assigned must at least be reasonably related to a person's position and qualifications. This does not mean that an administrative assistant may have to make a determination on acquiring a certain client, but it does mean that a vice president may have to change the toner in a copier machine. Where an assistant's duties are concerned, everything the assistant can do, other staff can do, too. More importantly, there are times when other staff should do it, too.

Certainly, others may be required to perform certain administrative tasks in emergency situations, but this expectation should become a requirement when time is a factor. When someone else can complete an administrative-related task faster than it would take to find or wait for the admin, then it is likely something that person ought to go ahead and complete. What prevents this is non-support staff viewing the performance of support duties as demeaning or beneath them. These duties are not. It actually compels an office to work more efficiently because it forces an office to work as a team. It inspires the attitude, *me for you and you for me,* which is missing in many offices. If I know that you do not value me or my work (position), then how willing do you think I will be to assist you—even when it *is* my job? Employers must distinguish between what an assistant's job is and what those things are they just do not want to do.

It is not fair to use other duties as assigned as a cop-out for avoiding unwanted work. It is even less fair to categorize that unwanted work as actual duties/responsibilities of the support staff only. Instead, office staff should treat all work as important. Whatever someone has to do—from answering the switchboard and disconnecting equipment to reconciling invoices and processing payroll—it should be respected.

Attachment Six

Double Standards

Treat all as your own self. Do not have a double standard.[22]

- Sri Sathya Sai Baba

[22] Baba, Sri Sathya Sai. "Sri Sathya Sai Baba Quotes." Think Exist.Com. Accessed March 25, 2013. http://thinkexist.com/quotation/treat-all-as-your-own-self-do-not-have-a-double/350661.html.

CONTEXT

When I took the job with Trully & Associates, unbeknownst to me, I was pregnant. It wasn't long after I began working that I began a period of regularly missing work for doctor's appointments. Even though my reason for missing a lot of work was quite legitimate, I still felt uncomfortable being gone so frequently, especially since I had just been hired.

I waited until the end of a pay period before putting myself on your calendar to speak with you about changing my schedule. I asked you if I could begin an alternative work schedule (AWS). Specifically, I asked if I could work nine-hour days, which would give me one eight-hour day and a regular day off (RDO), every other week. Of course, you were familiar with what I was requesting because half of the office worked an AWS. The only rule was that we coordinate our RDO so that someone from each department was in the office on any given day.

There was some hesitancy on your part to approve this type of schedule for me—and by now, you know I'm about to talk about that—but you did, and I was thrilled! I was also thrilled that for the most part, my doctor's office obliged my request to schedule many of my appointments on my RDO so I could use as little leave as possible.

***** ***** *****

This arrangement worked out well. For a little over three months, there was not one problem with my absences. It was a Friday when I came to see you about a leave request I had just entered into PALACE. When I walked into your office and saw Gordon in there, I motioned that I would come back later.

"No, it's okay. Come on in." I was hoping Gordon would excuse himself, but he didn't.

"I just sent you a leave request for next Tuesday. I have a doctor's appointment in the morning and another appointment in the afternoon."

"Next Tuesday?" Gordon turned around in his seat to face me.

For a number of reasons, I ignored him: I was not talking to him; he was no longer my supervisor, so he did not have to approve my leave; and I WASN'T TALKING TO HIM!

He turned to you and repeated himself. "Next Tuesday?"

"Yes," you answered.

"But next Wednesday is the Energy Summit," he looked concerned.

And then suddenly, so did you. "That's right." You moved some papers on your desk and looked closely at your desk calendar. "Do you have to be out next Tuesday? We're going to be really busy preparing for Wednesday."

"Unfortunately, I can't reschedule the appointments. Both are already rescheduled dates."

You glanced again at your calendar. "And wait, you're already going to be out on Monday, aren't you? Isn't Monday your RDO?"

DISCUSSION

At that moment, I do not know what I hated more—the fact that Gordon was there or that you were grilling me about another especially sensitive issue. Easily, this entire memorandum is a list of the many double standards shown toward people in a support position. While they fall under many categories, the most common involves leave and absences from work.

No one—in my experience, anyway—gets as much grief as my position does when we go missing from work. And by work, I mean our "post." Even before we are absent from the office, if we are only away from our desks, all hell breaks loose. It does not matter why we are not at our desks—we could be in the bathroom, at the FedEx drop box, delivering something to a staff member, cleaning up after a meeting, or just shooting the breeze at a friend's desk—if we are not sitting in our seats the moment certain people (namely managers) come looking for us, people become incensed! We are hunted down, interrogated, and made to feel like we have been goofing off somewhere because we were not at our desks *right then*. When we are out of the office all together, though, the response is even more dramatic.

When I retold the incident of the failed conference call, I specifically described how Justin was not available on any of the Friday dates when polling staff for their availability. You and I laughed about this because his regular absences on Fridays were common occurrences. People joked openly about never expecting to see him on a Friday. In fact, every Thursday around lunch time, people started talking about what excuse he would give as the reason he would not be in the office the next day.

It was such a joke that Gordon even chimed in.[23] Supposedly, after Justin called in because his water heater had burst, Gordon remarked that he had run out of family members to get sick, so he moved to home emergencies. Whatever his exact comment was, the point remained that everyone, including management, knew Justin regularly took Fridays off, but management never reprimanded him for this or gave him grief about it.

Now, I discussed previously that his outstanding performance might be one reason management would turn a blind eye to this otherwise inappropriate behavior. However, my point now is that despite his regular absences, he somehow still had enough leave to take *at least* two, two-week vacations every year! I was always curious about the amount of leave he had, and I got my answer the first time I filled in for Cecilia and had to reconcile time and attendance.

Justin was able to take so much time off because he never used leave for any of his *slick* days. *Never*! Yes, he was the managing director, but did that make his blatant misuse of leave acceptable? Purely out of spite, I brought my discovery to his attention.

"Hey, Justin," I started when I entered his office. "You know I'm doing the LDR[24] for Cecilia while she's out, and I just have a quick question." I watched his eyebrow rise. "I know that you were out last Friday, and I believe the Friday before that, as well. But I didn't see a leave request in the system for that time."

For effect, I paused a few seconds. "You know I don't do this all the time, so I don't know. But are managers using some other leave request system?"

---

[23] Actually, he only told Brandy, but she told Jacob and he told me.

[24] Leave distribution report.

I could have been nominated for an Academy Award—though I might have been beaten out by his face alone. It was somewhere between incredulousness and anger. Whatever it was, I knew that he knew what I was getting at.

When he began to run down the evenings he stayed late in order to make up the hours, I was surprised. I felt a little bad, even. I had nothing against Justin, absolutely no authority to do anything about it, and beyond trying to make a point, I didn't care! While I knew he was lying about having made up those hours, my point was that there was no way Jacob or I could have gotten away with that.

I know because we tried.

In fact, just the week prior, Jacob had somewhat of a run-in with Gordon behind this very thing. Thursday of that week, he stayed an hour late to finish some preparations for a meeting. That Friday, he left an hour early for his doctor's appointment.

The following week, after Cecilia had given Gordon the LDR report to approve, he came to see Jacob.

"Jacob, you don't have a leave request in PALACE for the hour you left early last week."

"I know. I worked an hour late on Thursday, so I didn't have to use my leave."

He chuckled. "Oh, no, who told you that you could make up time like that?" Jacob attempted to answer, but Gordon continued. "You left early. You weren't here. How do you figure you shouldn't use leave for that?"

JERK! What he figured was that since everyone else could do it, he could, too! He worked an hour late. He left an hour early. What was the big deal? Gordon was grilling him like there was an 8-hour discrepancy or like he had claimed overtime hours that he had not worked.

Brandy had just given the exact same excuse—in the middle of a staff meeting, no less. She traipsed into the meeting 15 minutes late (which made her an hour-and-a-half late to work, mind you), took her seat, and began sipping her coffee. During our individual department/work reports, Cecilia—who was not a fan of Brandy's—announced that she would be reconciling leave and processing payroll, and she reminded everyone to turn in their timesheets before noon.

"Don't worry, Brandy. I don't need you to submit leave in PALACE for this morning's hour-and-a-half. I'll go ahead and record it for you."

Jacob and I proceeded to kick each other under the table. I thought Brandy might accidentally spit out her coffee. Both she and Gordon exchanged quick glances, and she spoke.

"I'll talk to you off-line, Cecilia. Because I worked late last week and had earned some comp time."

Comp time, my ass! First of all, remaining ten minutes beyond your regular time each day to change into your tennis shoes, empty your water container, and basically just *lollygag* until your boss can see that you are "still in the office" does not constitute working late. Neither does shuffling and reshuffling papers, moving paper piles from one side of your desk to the other. Brandy made much noise "working" late, but she never worked on anything. She didn't even work during regular hours, which is why she always had piles and piles of paper on her desk to move in the first place!

But I have digressed, slightly. My point is that she was never forced to use leave. I know this because while I had Cecilia's LDR reports and files, I went back through previous reports and looked at what *everybody* had going on in the leave department.

Pray tell what made Brandy's excuse legitimate but not Jacob's? I know why management would feel within their right to carry on this way, but Brandy was not management. So the fact that she could get away with doing this while Jacob and I could not was simply not fair.

I stood in your office looking to *use* my leave, and I was still receiving grief. Believe me, I know my timing was inopportune. We did have an important meeting the following day, so I absolutely understood your concern. However, I still tried to get you to see we were already in good shape for that meeting. I explained that the materials had already been taken to the copy center, lunch had already been ordered, and the signs had been made. I told you that Jacob and I had finished the name badges and tent cards for those who had pre-registered that morning (110 people).

Of course, there would be jackasses who would call at the last minute to attend, forcing last-minute badges and other changes, but nothing would have come up that Monday or Tuesday that Jacob could not handle alone. We had already ordered extra lunch and made extra copies of the handouts. And even still, he and I had a lot of experience handling last-minute things the morning of a meeting, too. My absence the day before this meeting, poorly timed as it was, would not have been as greatly felt as your concern implied, if felt at all.

"I just don't understand why you can't reschedule this appointment for Thursday, Leslie. Or even Friday. Can you see if you can at least get something for Wednesday afternoon?"

Again, I know the timing was not ideal, so I understood why you did not want to approve the leave. At this point, however, your grilling me pissed me off. Was Justin or Brandy ever grilled like this when they wanted to take time off? Suppose I had not requested the day off in advance in the first place? What if I had called in sick instead? You would not have been able to do anything about me being absent then, so what was the difference?

"Joyce, this caught me off guard as well," I continued with my lies. "If you want, I can come in on Monday and switch my RDO to Tuesday just for next week, but either way, I have to keep this appointment on Tuesday."

Other times, when I asked to be off and you felt it was not convenient, I had always been able to "win you over" by being caught up with my work. I could explain to you where I stood on all of my projects, and you were satisfied. I really do believe the only reason you gave me the third degree was because Gordon was in your office—especially since you stuck to your guns in his presence, but shortly after he left, e-mailed me to tell me to go ahead and take both days.[25]

[25] I was relieved when I saw that email because I didn't have to feel bad about calling in sick . . . because I sure was going to.

COMPROMISE

The term "double standard" is defined as "a standard or rule that is unfairly applied to some people only." A second definition adds that it is also an "*expectation* that is applied unfairly to different groups, one group usually being condemned for the slightest offense while the other is treated far more leniently."[26] When employers employ double standards, they are essentially breeding office pets, and this is the first thing that should be avoided if you want to have a happier, more successful office.

Avoiding Office Pets

The danger of office pets is more logical than most employers probably know. When people—from office workers or maintenance workers to busboys or bus drivers—are rewarded regularly when they have not merited a reward, they *will* eventually feel rules and expectations do not apply to them. When people can enjoy certain perks and benefits they have not earned, they *will* eventually feel they do not have to perform well, or perform at all, because there will be no penalty, anyway. The fact that it eventually affects performance is what should concern employers the most.

Ordinarily, each program manager was responsible for providing committee updates to you or Gordon, which you then presented during the board meeting. Brandy had been *tasked* with also sending Gordon the information for a subcommittee meeting she had held with one of Gordon's committees. During the preceding staff meeting, Gordon told her to pull together the info, add it to her regular committee update, and send him one file with the complete information.

[26] Microsoft Word Reference Books. "Double Standard." Accessed March 25, 2013.

"When did you want that by, Gordon," she asked, unaware that everyone else had begun giving each other crazy looks across the table.

We knew the question was dumb because board meeting reports were always due to you and Gordon the Friday before the board meeting. Already, Brandy was displaying why office pets are dangerous. She was allowed to be a discombulated, disconnected dummy, not as involved in committee and office work as she should have been. She did not even know when certain reports were due—reports that were due the same time every quarter since Trully & Associates existed.

"This Friday," Gordon answered her.

"Okay," she replied and made a notation on her Hello Kitty notepad.

She did send the information on the Friday it was due, but what took place after that, I know you remember well. The week of the meeting, that Monday, she scooted out early behind Gordon who left early behind a family emergency. She called in *slick* the next day, more than likely because she knew Gordon would still be out because of his emergency, which he was. What she missed on her poorly timed slick day was Gordon's email to you that he would be out for the entire week and that Brandy would give the report to the board on his behalf.

Though she missed the email that day, she might have seen it the next morning and still had time to prepare for it had she come in on time. By the time she waltzed in her usual hour-and-a-half late, that agenda item had come and gone. But for the fact I was cleaning up the breakfast and other mess left from the meeting, I would have missed the director cussing you out because that information had not been presented. And worse, you knew nothing about it to even adlib a summary.

The moment the last board member left, you practically sprinted down the hall to her office. I do not know if she had seen the email by then and was aware of the catastrophe she caused, but by the time you finished going up one side of her and down the other, the entire floor was aware.

When you were finished, she had the nerve to remark, "Well, when Gordon emailed you yesterday to tell you he was putting me on the agenda, you should have told him then that I wasn't here. Or you should have called me at home to tell me I was being put on the agenda."

"First of all, I didn't know you were out yesterday. I don't know who is here and who isn't on a daily basis. It's not my job to keep track of individuals and when they're in or out. Second, you had a whole hour to prepare something this morning, Brandy!" You were yelling again then. "The meeting didn't start until 9:15."

"I didn't get here until 9:30. Gordon knows I like to see my son get on the school bus, so some mornings, I'm late. But I always stay to make up that time."

"Get your stuff and leave this office, now. You're fired!" That would have been *my* response to her, but you remained as professional as you could (I guess) and told her to put herself and Gordon on your calendar as soon as Gordon was back in the office because the conversation was not over.

But for the fact you were caught in the crosshairs of the "pet monster" Gordon created in Brandy, I wonder if my point here would have been lost on you. Despite the example I just gave, however, having favorites in an office is not bad entirely. If anyone can be special and receive preferential treatment, it should at least be the person who performs well and not the person who holds a certain position.

Performance-Based versus Position-Based Treatment

Let me begin by saying that the most obvious exception to giving position-based treatment is management. If anyone is entitled to a little preferential treatment, management is. Executives do not just wake up one day on top of the corporate ladder.[27] They reach this pinnacle after years of hard work, studying their field, making business decisions and choosing business relationships, and shedding a whole lot of sweat and tears.

Minus the paycheck, I do not envy people in management. Outside of the administrative staff, you have the most stressful job imaginable. The weight of the entire company rests ultimately on your shoulders. The decisions you make, make or break a company. You do not have to make a mistake yourself, but if the people under the people under the people under you mess up badly enough, the finger can be pointed all the way back up to you. Especially with giant organizations and companies, *your* job can be demanded for the failures of people you did not hire, personally interview, conduct background checks on, etc. Your head can be required because you are the owner, president, director, or CEO, and well, *somebody* has to take the fall.

Even I think this is a lot to contend with, so a larger office with a beautiful view, expensive furniture, and a private bathroom—that's nothing. You deserve that! You have earned parking spaces closest to the building, expense accounts, and executive secretaries

[27] There are exceptions to this, as well, but for the purposes of this memorandum, I am not discussing those executives who achieved that status by means such as sleeping their way to the top, benefiting from nepotism, etc.

with responsibilities more like personal assistants.[28] And in all sincerity, you are worthy of the net that is deposited into your bank accounts each and every payday!

However, your entitlement to special treatment and perks such as these does not give you the right to treat others differently based on position. The rules and codes of conduct that management must abide by are rightly different from those that non-management must follow, but the buck stops there. ALL other employees, including support employees, should have the same rules and expectations and be evaluated against the same principles of conduct. Again, if you have to treat people differently at all, surely you see the value in basing that treatment on performance.

I said earlier that when I wanted to do something (like take a day off in the middle of a busy period), many times, even though you might not have wanted me to, I could usually win you over by being caught up with my work. If you had everything you needed for a meeting, if I had no outstanding reports to complete, if there was literally nothing pressing going on that I had to handle, why wouldn't you be willing to impart some leniency on me? If I was asking every week to leave early or come in late, using the same excuse, then I could understand your unwillingness. Yet, I regularly performed above your and other people's expectations . . . for no reward.

I could never get you to understand that rewarding me (or anyone else for that matter) for performing well was to your benefit, as well. Increased productivity (and employee morale) is a direct effect of small gestures like allowing employees to go home early more frequently (see Appendix). In fact, it is a wise reward for the hard-working employee.

---

[28] Food for the executive's thought: even though you are entitled to certain privileges, is there a point when even your entitlements become excessive? (Here's a hint: YES!)

If an office has had a trying, busy week and on a Friday finds itself in a bit of a work lull, letting employees leave early becomes a great reward. It becomes a way of saying thanks and showing appreciation for a job well done. Everyone knows that receiving rewards compels the recipient to repeat the behavior—in this case, hard work—in order to receive the reward again.

On the other hand, if we do not reap any benefit for our hard work, how hard do you think employees will work? Yes, we are supposed to work hard and perform solidly regardless. You said on more than one occasion that my paycheck was already my reward, but if you had sent me home early once a week, you would have been surprised at how much more cooperative I would have been.

If you had sent me home early for setting up a conference room adequately, you would have been surprised even more at how the preparation for all of your meetings had improved. If you had sent me home early or let me take off to get a jump on long weekends, get ahead of traffic and impending bad weather, or just because you were in a good mood—showing that you cared about my personal and mental health—I would have shown you just how much I could care about the health of the organization. I believe the main reason for your hesitancy, besides not basing it on my performance, was the grief you often got behind my being out of the office, period.

We know, and it has been discussed previously, the impact on an office when support staff, in particular, is short. People who are not usually the receptionist or secretary's back up are annoyed with having to answer the phones.[29] Someone who would have ordinarily changed the toner or replaced the paper in the copier

---

[29] The people who *are* the usual back up are annoyed, too, a point that has already been addressed.

without a problem suddenly has a problem on the day that I am out.

Simple tasks somehow become complicated. Every machine picks that day to break and stop working. Every report, notebook, key, file, etc. that is always on my desk, visible, suddenly vanishes, and no one can find anything. Phones that normally rarely ring suddenly ring off the hook, and no one could get any work done. Yes, everything always goes awry when the support person is out.

Please! With few exceptions, the day or days when I was out of the office were no different than the days when I was there. Instead, people whined and complained about every little inconvenience—real or imagined—so that my absence appeared to have something to do with my performance. Where the issue of leave is concerned, in particular, employers should remember that all employees have the right to be absent from work, even support employees whose absences are not as badly felt as people believe (or as people act).

The Right to Request

Just like JG Wentworth's commercial declares, "It's my money and I need it now," it's my leave, and if I want to use it "now," I can! I have worked the eight, nine, or however many hours and earned it, so I can use it whenever I want. Denying use of leave that I have earned or been given is the equivalent of saying you control when I can be seen by my doctor or dentist—that you can dictate when I tend to home or other personal emergencies or when I can take my vacations and other personal time—and you cannot!

We all remember the unfortunate events with Kathleen's daughter when she left her abusive ex-husband. Kathleen shared the entire ordeal with us—the 911 emergency phone calls, the restraining orders, the custody battle, his threats, and even the scare when it appeared he had kidnapped their son. We went through this with her, but she also went through months of sporadic absences. She would be in the middle of a meeting and have to leave immediately for something else that had happened.

Everyone was remorseful for her situation. Even when you grew a little less "patient," I'll say, you never denied her leave or harassed her about making up the time. Now, without sounding like a complete jerk, what really was the difference between that situation and mine? Surely, you are not saying I have to be experiencing something as tragic as Kathleen's ordeal in order to be "excused," are you?

I know there are seasons, if you will, in offices when the workload can be really busy and employers prefer all hands on deck, but that is really all it is—a preference. I cannot predict and pre-plan everything that may require time out of the office any more than you have a right to tell me when I can and cannot take off. Any employee in good standing has a right to request/use leave, and contrary to many managers' opinions, it cannot always be dependent upon work obligations. Even when employees try to be mindful of meetings, busy times, and other work activities and schedule their vacations and personal time around that, they are still mistreated. This can sometimes lead them to develop a *why bother* attitude.

I will never forget my second winter here—specifically the staff meeting where you asked everyone to get their leave and vacation plans to me by COB so I could generate the holiday calendar for you. You went into this long spiel about your family's upcoming trip to Italy for the Christmas holiday.

"This will be the first time we'll have all five generations together," you yakkity yapped. "We're going to have a professional oil painting done while standing on the Ponte Vittorio Emanuele. We learned that a distant relative of my family is Ennio De Rossi, the architect whose designs this bridge is based on."[30]

Eventually, you concluded that you and Gordon would both be out that Monday, but Gordon would be back in the office that Tuesday. "George will be acting on Monday."

Suddenly, George shifted in his seat. "Uhh, Joyce, I put in for that same week. My family and I are going to Disneyworld for the holiday."

"Oh," was your unenthusiastic reply.

He went on to explain that he had requested that time off a month-and-a-half-ago, and you had already approved it. You held the staff meeting up for several minutes "teasing" him about always being in the office the week of Christmas. "You never go anywhere. Now I have the family trip of the century and you want to go see Mickey!"

"I know," he tried smiling. "But we have the two grandbabies now, so we're going to try a trip to Disneyworld—driving down and everything."

George could not even get feigned interest from you, after he sat patiently through your tale of Italian travels and ancestry and photo shoots on top of a damn bridge. Just like you said, he was always in the office—and not just during the week of Christmas. He was your and Gordon's regular "acting manager" because he was always at work, but now he was getting the cold shoulder because what? You made an assumption!

[30] Dude, nobody cares about that except your family! If you're going to broadcast your money and means, which far exceed that of the rest of your staff, DON'T! Least of all during a staff meeting!

George later shared with Jacob and me that while he had put the request in for the time off, he had not paid for any part of the trip, yet. They were only staying at his timeshare, and he and his family would have had no problem changing the week. Behind your unappreciative response, however, he kept his plans. (And to nobody's surprise, so did you and Gordon. I do not remember who ended up acting in George's place, but it clearly was not an issue who did. So why make George feel badly for daring to be out of the office when he usually wasn't, and when you, Gordon, and *the rest of the working world* took time off, too?)

SUMMARY

"What's good for the goose is good for the gander" is indeed a cliché, but its truth for the office is paramount. It is very hard to justify applying a different set of rules or expectations for one group of employees and not another. Generally, the determining factor is position, and this is not fair. Positions that are esteemed as higher or more important are allowed more leniencies than those regarded as less important. Thus, it is easy to begin treating the people in those positions differently, and this is not merely unfair—it is dangerous.

Employees who regularly receive rewards, even when they are unmerited, will develop behavior that is detrimental to an office: failure to perform; failure to perform well; failure to accept responsibility for poor performance; and maybe even failure to answer to management and abide by any rules. The employee who is never rewarded (or rewarded less frequently) may become a liability, as well, and develop resentment and anger toward management, or the preferred employee, that can boil over into more detrimental behavior.

If employers insist on having office pets, it should at least be the person who performs the greatest, even if it is a support employee. Love may make the world go 'round, but rewarding outstanding performance makes an office stay afloat. Some of the rewards should be pay raises, promotions, etc., but employers should also consider other temporary rewards that can have the same positive effect, including time off and a more lenient leave policy.

There is no perfect time for office employees to be out, so at least appreciate the staff who attempt to be mindful of work obligations and adjust their leave requests accordingly. Where support employees are concerned, remember that everyone has a right to take off, even if the timing is not ideal in the mind of management.

Trully & Associates

Trully & Associates
1548 New Birth Street, NW
Third Floor
Washington, DC 20096

~~Employee~~ Manager Performance Review

~~Employee~~ Manager Information

Name	Joyce M. Trully	**Employee ID**	N/A
Job Title	President & CEO	**Date**	April 25, 2013
Department	N/A	**~~Manager~~ Employee**	Leslie D. Lewis
Review Period	April 24, 2012 – April 25, 2013		

Ratings

	1 = Poor	2 = Fair	3 = Satisfactory	4 = Good	5 = Excellent
Job Knowledge	☐	☐	☐	☐	☒
Comments	You possess a keen sense of business. Your ability to choose member companies to expand the impact of Trully & Associates is commendable.				
Work Quality	☐	☐	☐	☐	☒
Comments	Your organization skills are exceptional.				
Attendance/Punctuality	☐	☐	☐	☐	☒
Comments	You rarely take time off and are a constant, regular fixture in the office, no matter the season.				
Initiative	☐	☐	☒	☐	☐
Comments	The initiative you take in growing the organization as a whole should be the same taken in growing employee relationships. Increasing employee morale, especially among support employees, matters as much as increasing business relationships.				
Communication/Listening	☐	☒	☐	☐	☐
Comments	Certain matters are often brought to your attention to handle, but they are dismissed and ignored. Your ability to listen to every employee and seek to resolve issues more effectively needs improvement.				
Cooperation	☒	☐	☐	☐	☐
Comments	As related to communication and listening skills, your ability and willingness to promote teamwork and collaboration amongst all employees needs improvement.				
Overall Rating *(average the rating numbers above)*	3.5				

Evaluation

ADDITIONAL COMMENTS	Overall, you are an exceptional chief executive officer. The manner in which you utilize managerial employees within the organization to further your business goals is impressive, but it is also very exclusive. It does not consider the presence and needs of all employees. If you dedicate an equal amount of time to understanding and listening to every employee, you may find the organization can grow even more.
GOALS *(as agreed upon by employee and manager)*	Institute a regular meeting with non-executive employees to gain a better understanding of the organization from their perspective. Change business operations accordingly.

Verification of Review

By signing this form, you confirm that you have discussed this review in detail with your ~~supervisor~~ employee. Signing this form does not necessarily indicate that you agree with this evaluation.

Employee Signature		Date	April 25, 2013
Manager Signature		Date	

Appendix

The Benefit of Frequent Early Dismissal (An Opinion Piece)

The desire to be dismissed early from work frequently might sound like something a poor-performing, lazy employee would request. On the contrary, if employers did it more frequently, they would find it has a direct, positive effect on many behaviors they find frustrating.

Less Leave Use

A lot of employers believe the frequency with which some employees "use" leave is more like "abusing" leave. Everyone in an office is affected when staff is short, and no time is that more frustrating than when it is last-minute and unexpected. If you are prepared to be short-handed, then you are just that—prepared. However, when you have projects to be finished and a significant number of people "out" suddenly, delegating and reassigning tasks can be frustrating. On top of that, you must also contend with the knowledge that half of those who are out are out for reasons you know are lies.

Every manager knows when employees are being slick. All it takes is for a little snow to fall and phone calls flood your voicemail about people not being able to get out of their driveways, off their streets, etc. People, I think, watch and wait for others to get sick and then take a slick day themselves under the guise that something is going around. I was overjoyed when I had my kids because then I could use the excuse that there was an emergency at my child's daycare in order to leave early, or I could say my child was sick as an excuse to miss work. Many times, my child was "sick," and I was home catching up on sleep, catching a sale at some store, catching a movie that had just come out, jumping on an early date with my husband, or just out enjoying a beautiful weather day!

There were times when I did not even try to disguise my leave "abuse." I told my supervisor often that I needed to leave early or come in late for a doctor's appointment and walked in with my hair freshly done! Everyone lies about the need for leave sometimes, and unfortunately, management cannot do a thing about it.

You cannot prove I did not go to the doctor's office and then go get my hair done. Perhaps, I was in route when they called and needed to reschedule my appointment, so *then* I went to get my hair done.

Unless you go to an employee's home, you cannot confirm that snow or ice really was not a problem. Whether an employee is lying or not, on some level, management has to suck up ALL leave use. HOWEVER, if you dismissed employees early more regularly, they could more honestly accomplish personal errands and take care of personal business without having to lie and without needing to use leave and miss a day of work. If you let us go home early, perhaps we can get a same-day appointment at the doctor, dentist, or hairdresser and won't have to call in. If employees are legitimately sick and happen to be in the middle of a busy period, letting them go home early might give them the opportunity to nurse that oncoming cold and prevent it from becoming full-blown—putting them out when their presence is especially critical.

Practicality

I should probably note here that letting employees go home early does not mean 30 minutes before the regular closing time. Now, lest I sound ungrateful for employers doing this at all, let me say I am not. However, this gift can be inadvertently undermined because the "early" part is not emphasized. Employees are much more likely to remember, appreciate, and respond more positively to a two-hour, or more, early dismissal than they are a *mere* 30 minutes.

The practicality of this gesture is especially felt around the holidays, particularly between Thanksgiving and New Year's. Most offices are empty—ghost towns—as a majority of staff are on leave. There are always the do-gooders in the office who still want to work, but even they do not have a lot to do because staff in the organizations with which they conduct business are out, too. So everyone everywhere is pretty much twiddling their thumbs.

Some employers attempt other gifts around this time such as allowing employees to dress down every day, bring in movies, openly play games, etc. After a few hours, however, even these freedoms lose their redeeming qualities because I can stay at home and do nothing all day. As much as watching movies or playing games is fun while at work—it is not fun for eight or nine straight hours. Around about the fourth or fifth hour, I am not thrilled that I had to get up early, take a shower, put on clothes, burn gas, and spend money on the subway, bus, or parking—just to sit and do nothing or pretend to be doing something. Then, it is not fun. It's stupid, so it is practical just to send us home early.

Frankly, there should be a federal or labor law requirement that all companies, during the more commonly slow periods of the year, regularly allow employees to go home early. I know the government, in particular, uses the excuse that its employees are being paid for a certain number of hours, and if employees do not work that number of hours, then we are scheming against the United States Federal Government—which is illegal. Um, aren't we doing that anyway by coming into the office and not working (because there is no work, not even busy work), but still logging eight hours on our timesheet—which implies we have worked on assignments for that full eight hours? JUST SEND US HOME AND STOP BEING RIDICULOUS!

Increased Productivity, Good Behavior, and Good Moods

Finally, allowing employees to go home more frequently directly affects employee morale, good behavior, and productivity—things that every good employer seeks to have. Allowing employees to leave early is actually a wise reward for hard work. If an office has had a trying, busy week, and on a Friday, finds itself in a bit of a work lull, letting employees leave early becomes a great reward. It becomes a way of saying thanks and showing appreciation for a job well done, and everyone knows that receiving rewards compels the recipient to repeat the behavior—in this case, hard work—in order to receive the reward again.

On the other hand, if we do not reap any benefit for our hard work, then how hard do you think we will work? Yes, we are supposed to work hard regardless, and it has been said that employees' paychecks are already their reward. But send your staff home early once a week and see how much more cooperative they become.

If a manager has had his fill of complaining, lying, poor-performing employees, send them home early every Friday and see how quickly their attitude toward work changes. Send them home early for setting up a conference room adequately, and see how the preparation for all of your meetings soon improves. Send all of your employees home early to get a jump on long weekends, to get ahead of traffic and impending bad weather, or just because you're in a good mood. Show that you care about their personal, mental health and see how much they begin to care about the health of the organization.

For every employee for whom this formula will work, I know there are some who will continue to lie, continue to abuse leave, not work any harder, etc. Those, you just need to fire because they are killing my point!

3432725R00072

Made in the USA
San Bernardino, CA
01 August 2013